D1297431

# Reddo's Raiders

*Memoirs of a B17 Bomber Aircraft Commander
during his tour with the 8th Air Force in World War II*

By

## James J. "Reddo" Redmond, Jr.
### Major, USAF Retired Reserve

© 2003 by James J. "Reddo" Redmond, Jr.  All rights reserved.

No part of this book may be reproduced, stored in a retrieval
system, or transmitted by any means, electronic, mechanical,
photocopying, recording, or otherwise, without written permission
from the author.

ISBN: 1-4140-3113-0 (e-book)
ISBN: 1-4140-3114-9 (Paperback)
ISBN: 1-4140-3115-7 (Dust Jacket)

This book is printed on acid free paper.

1stBooks - rev. 12/10/03

*This book is dedicated to
the men and women who fought during World War II;
those that survived and
those that did not.
Your valiant efforts will never be forgotten.*

*A special thank you to Christine C. Wickham and
Elizabeth C. Sullivan for their assistance with this work.*

# TABLE OF CONTENTS

# INTRODUCTION

The story told here is a true recount of the life and happenings of a B-17 bomber pilot and his crew from the start of war in Europe in 1939 to the end of hostilities. This presentation is made in four sections, the first of which is concerned primarily with the period from September 1939 to December 1943. This is the period during which the crew was formed, trained and made ready for combat.

The second section is devoted to combat with the Eighth Air Force in the Air Offensive over Germany and Occupied Europe. The material comprising this reporting was provided by diaries maintained by the author as supplemented by contributions from members of his crew. This crew flew 34 combat missions during their membership in the 509th Squadron of the 351st Bomb Group while stationed at Polebrook, England from December 1943 to July 1944.

The third section consists of a sequence of letters between the author and Lloyd Bogle, the crew's radio operator. There are about 30 letters and each brings up an instance or occurrence relating to combat and the reply comments on this and raises new issues. These letters are presented as they were written with no attempt to correct grammar or punctuation.

The last section presents a series of vignettes describing various aspects of life as a combat crewman in the Eighth Air Force during World War II. Also included are some combat statistics and a few poems and writings relating to the Eighth Air Force combat.

# SECTION ONE

## SEPTEMBER 3, 1939 to 1958

I was still in school with the start of war in Europe in September 1939. I was beginning my sophomore year at Canisius College in Buffalo, New York and just finishing my summer employment as a third helper in the open hearth furnaces of the Bethlehem Steel Company. The commencement of hostilities of war in Europe were of interest to me, but concerned me not at all. It was a foreign war and none of our business. During these years in college, in addition to maintaining a passing grade, I participated in all social activities and was a member of both the track team and the boxing team. During my junior year I was the light weight boxing champion of my college conference and a member of the class football team which was undefeated during our sophomore, junior and senior years. I was enjoying my college career and it was in my senior year that I started to think seriously about flying.

On the Sunday afternoon of December 7, 1941 I had a date with my girl, Jayne that included dinner at her home with her parents. Traveling towards her home I was thinking how great life was. I was twenty-one years old and in a few months I would have my BBA degree (Bachelor of Business Administration degree). The world was there to conquer. With the self confidence and arrogance of youth, I felt ready for anything but I had not considered war. Then, like a bolt from the blue, the radio delivered its ominous message. Pearl Harbor had been attacked and bombed by Japan. Although I had no idea what Pearl Harbor was, or where it was, I knew it was part of America, and that this meant war.

1

*James J. "Reddo" Redmond, Jr.*

Dinner at Jayne's home with her parents had always been a pleasant and jovial occasion. This dinner turned out to be different from all the others. There was tension brought on by the bombing of Pearl Harbor that shrouded the usual good time. Jayne's parents were concerned about her older brother who had been called into the army as a result of the peace time draft. We were now going into a war with Japan and only an hour earlier my plans and dreams were concerned with Jayne, my studies, flying, and generally having a good time. Little did I know that for the next half dozen years my life would be flying, combat and war.

One of my first exposures to what World War II would mean to me, was when my cousin Bob Carroll went into the Marines. Bob, after graduation from College, had taught for several years at Lackawanna High south of Buffalo. While not true now, in those depression years, teaching was a much sought after career. He had secured his tenure and returned to academia, entering the University of Buffalo Law School. Then came the peace time draft. He came up with one of the highest numbers chosen. Since he was already so far along in his pursuit of a law degree, he was accorded several deferments. In the spring of 1942, we were at war and with only a few months to graduation, the draft board refused any further deferments. It seemed to me totally unreasonable for the draft board to refuse a deferment of three months to allow for completion of his law degree. Faced with the draft, Bob elected to enlist in the Marines as a private since he was six months too old to qualify for OCS (Officer's Candidate School).

After a short time as a DI (Drill Instructor), the age restriction was raised and he was accepted into OCS. On graduating from OCS, he was commissioned and assigned to over seas duty. He participated in several island campaigns, being wounded on Saipan and again on Iwo Jima. He survived the war, but with a piece of shrapnel imbedded in his head which could not be removed. He did return to his studies and received his law degree.

2

Although my inclusion of this brief reference to Bob Carroll's experience with the draft board and the military is not really part of this story, it is pertinent to revealing the atmosphere in which I lived.

All through my growing up years, I would, whenever I felt the need, have what might be described as "Father-Son Talks" with my father. There was no pattern to when they occurred; they took place whenever I felt the need.

I don't remember what the subject of most of these talks was. They were probably very juvenile. One subject that I remember very well was discussed several times during my senior year in college. It had to do with flying and military service. I was now learning to fly and had hopes of becoming an army pilot. During this period, the accomplishments of the American Volunteer Group, better known as the Flying Tigers were every day news in the papers. Their experiences in China, in combat with the Japanese were exciting. I was enthralled with them, and would discuss them with my father. If I had been finished with college and been a qualified pilot, I would have volunteered to be one of them. I would burden my father with my dreams and goals of becoming an Army Air Corps pilot. My father would encourage me and he never threw cold water on anything even if he thought it was beyond accomplishment.

A year and a half later, when I was being graduated from flying school, my dad spoke quietly to me, referring to our talks, that when I was telling him about my intentions to become an Army Air Corps pilot; he hoped I could follow my dreams. He also mentioned that he knew how difficult a course I had planned and he did not want me disappointed. I was totally surprised that he remembered our talks so well and that he took them so seriously.

At the time war was declared, the government was offering a new program to college students called C.P.T. (Civilian Pilot Training) Program. In order to be accepted (in addition to meeting requirements for scholastic standing and passing the physical examinations), it was necessary to agree that upon request; you would volunteer for training as an Aviation Cadet. I agreed, was accepted, entered the program, and went on to earn my private pilot's license.

As my college graduation approached, I had received my private pilot's license, and knew that my grades assured me of graduation on schedule. Life was flowing on smoothly. In the middle of May 1942, I received a letter from the government reminding me of the training I had received in the C.P.T. Program and of the promise I had given to volunteer for the Cadets, if and when I was requested. The letter went on stating that I was hereby requested to volunteer no later than June 10, 1942. I went to the recruiting office and volunteered for the Cadets, was accepted, and sworn in on June 1, 1942 as a private in the Army Air Corps Reserve. I was placed on inactive duty, and graduated from college on June 7, 1942.

Now that I had enlisted and was waiting for a call to active duty as an Aviation Cadet, I had little to do. I decided to return to Canisius and take a course in Physics. I thought this course would be very helpful in my aviation training. If I had known how difficult this course would be, I might not have taken it.

The course lasted six weeks. Five days a week we had class from 9:00 AM to 12:30 PM, and laboratory from 1:00 to 5:00 PM. In addition to this, homework was assigned that would require about two hours per night. Since I was not looking for credit and only wanted the knowledge the course would give me, I never once did the home work. I surprised myself by passing and getting credit for the course. Taking this course turned out to be very beneficial to me in my aviation training.

During the summer of 1942, it seemed that all my friends were being drafted or called to active duty and of course, each was given a farewell party. The summer of 1942 was a continuous round of parties although each subsequent party had missing members. By the time I was called to active duty, about twenty percent of the original group had left. I had a bet with one of my closest friends about who would be called to active duty first. I won.

The summer of 1942 passed into history with the bittersweet memories of the parties, and the uncertainty of when I might be called to active duty. On Saturday, September 3, 1942, my dad woke me to say there was what looked like a very important letter for me from the Army. Was it important? You bet! It ordered me to active duty effective that day, September 3, 1942, and ordered me to report in Nashville, Tennessee at 9:00 AM on Monday September 5, 1942. I had the rest of Saturday afternoon and all day Sunday until 7:00 PM to get ready to leave, say goodbye to my friends and get to the train station. There was no time for a goodbye party for me.

As ready as I thought I was, it seemed that I wasn't ready at all. There were dozens of things that had to be taken care of. The most important of these was my relationship with my girl, Jayne Aspden. We had been going steady for several years, and it was assumed mutually that we would eventually get married. The future, which had seemed so secure only a few months ago, was in disarray. Since the day of my enlistment I had been wrestling with the problem of whether I should let our relationship continue in absentia, or give Jayne the liberty to be a free young adult. I did not make up my mind until I was on my way to say goodbye to Jayne that Saturday night. It was terribly difficult, but I finally decided to end the exclusive relationship. We talked for an hour or two in my car parked in front of her house and when I left, Jayne had accepted our new relationship, although tearfully.

As bad as Jayne must have felt, I think I felt worse. I was in total depression as I drove home. I felt that I had lost a part of life. I had never thought that our relationship would come to an end in this manner. Depressed or not, I had to leave the next day, and start a new life. Jayne and I continued a relationship but on the basis of friendship rather than that of lovers. We corresponded regularly during my military career, with ever decreasing intimacy.

*James J. "Reddo" Redmond, Jr.*

Jayne eventually met and married a nice guy. I don't know whether he was in the military or if he was a feather merchant. I met him, but I could not say that I knew him.

One incident which I would like to recall happened the first Christmas that I was in the Cadets. Jayne wrote and asked what she could get me for Christmas, explaining that with my being in the military, she didn't know what I could use or would like. I had no real needs or requirements, but I had a real desire for a certain homemade cinnamon sucker made only on the lake shore. This candy manufacturer did a good business in the summer but I think was closed during the winter. The more I thought about these cinnamon suckers, I could almost taste them. I wrote Jayne reminding her of the candy manufacturer and asking her to get me fifty cinnamon suckers. She thought I was kidding, or maybe being a smart ass, but I convinced her that I was serious. I got my cinnamon suckers for Christmas. I hoarded these suckers and made them last for months. This was the best Christmas present I received.

It required a real effort for Jayne to get these suckers. First of all, Jayne did not drive. She had to get some one to drive her one hundred miles round trip to get them and I suspect she had to convince the manufacturer to make up a special order, because they are not open in the winter. Anyway, I really appreciated that Christmas present. It was one that I had no reason to expect, and one I would never forget.

Sunday night, when I was about ready to leave for the train, I had a discussion with my dad that went something like this: I told him that most parents broadcast the accomplishments of their sons. This I understood, but because of the toughness of the program I was entering into and the fact that only one in four complete the course and are rated as pilot I did not want any progress reports made on me with the chance that I might fail along the way. My father agreed even though it would be difficult to remain silent when friends might be talking or bragging about their sons. My father kept his word and there were no progress

6

reports made on me until the newspaper announced that I had won my wings.

There was one last piece of advice that my dad gave me as we departed for the train. He said, "I only ask that you never do anything that you would not feel free to do in my presence." I don't know whether I ever violated this or not, but it gave me problems from time to time because I never forgot it.

As the time drew close to my time for leaving, my parents were trying so hard to keep things normal, even though things were not normal at all. From my parent's point of view, they were losing a son. From my point of view, I was leaving on a great adventure, and couldn't wait to get started. My mother, who had been "keeping a stiff upper lip" did not want to go to the train station. I approved of that.

My dad drove me to the train station where I boarded the train for Nashville. After I had located my berth, I visited the lounge car where I met a Dr. Good. For most of the evening, we discussed the military and my upcoming career as a cadet. It must have been very profound because neither one of us knew what he was talking about. As the train made its way to Nashville, each stop brought a number of kids, all on the way to Nashville to join the cadet program.

The train arrived in Nashville at about 9:00 AM. It was mass confusion. None of the cadets knew what to do or where to go. Everybody was just milling around in the train station when some army personnel appeared and rounded up the cadets into trucks to transport us to the Classification Center. The Center was located about ten miles out of town and was a brand new facility. As we were being transported through the center on our way to our barracks, those cadets who had arrived a day or two before us would, on seeing us pass, come out of their barracks and yell in unison: "YOU'LL BE SORRY!" What a welcome!

The barracks were completed but not ready for occupancy. There was saw dust and wood shavings all over. It was obvious that the carpenters had just left. The bunks were still in cartons, and the mattresses were still in wrappings. Pillows and blankets were wrapped and stored in a big pile.

We were put to work cleaning up the barracks, setting up the bunks, and placing the mattresses, blankets and pillows. It took about half a day to get a barracks ready for occupancy. We would then be marched to a mess hall where we had lunch and then we were put to work setting up another barracks. This program lasted for several days until all the barracks were ready for the new cadets who were arriving.

After we finished with cleaning the barracks, we didn't have much to do, only odd jobs, talk to the other guys in the barracks and write letters. We didn't have much to write about. Nothing exciting had happened to us that would be worth writing about so this quickly became boring. This inactivity caused me to become homesick for the first time in my life. Thank goodness it passed in a day or two. The next thing for us was our shots. Generally they were not too bad, although one of them gave me a fever and the tetanus shot was a bugger. It made my arm feel as though it had been hit with a baseball bat. My arm was sore for several days.

Now we really got active. We were marched to an auditorium where we took classification tests to determine which Air Corps specialty we were best suited for: pilot, navigator or bombardier. About half the tests were concerned with mental acuity and half tested manual dexterity. The dexterity tests were fun, and the mental tests were frustrating. The mental tests were made very long and there was a strict time limit, so no one could finish. This prevented one from knowing how well he had done. The manual dexterity tests measured hand, eye and brain coordination. There were many interesting tests, but the one that remains vividly in memory was the one that tested nerves.

In this test, you were required to stand arm's length from a panel which had a small hole about the size of a pencil eraser. You were required to hold an instrument similar to an ice pick with the point in the center of the hole. If the point of the instrument touched the side of the hole, a buzzer would sound and a light would flash. The idea was to keep the pointer centered and not allow it to touch the sides of the hole. After we had been shown how it worked, someone read a passage which lasted about five minutes. The story which was read told how you have successfully completed cadet training and have been graduated as a pilot. Everything is going great. This was delivered in a very calm story telling way. Then the tempo increased. The story tells that you are having a successful military career and are now the pilot of a bomber and are in combat. The story which was so interesting that you could not resist listening now got emotional. The reader would scream, *"Fighters are attacking, your plane has been hit, your plane is on fire. WHAT WILL YOU DO? Men are wounded, they are screaming for help. WILL YOU CRACK UP?"* It seemed that whenever the reader screamed, your hand would tremble and the pointer would touch the side of the hole. When you pulled the pointer away from the side of the hole, it would slam into the other side of the hole. When this test was over, I was dripping with sweat.

The testing took three or four days, and after it was over no one had any idea as to the results. There was no news at all, not even a rumor. It was my introduction to a typical army procedure, wait and wonder.

Although all the cadets were strangers to each other, I had become friends with a cadet named George Quinlan. We were alphabetically next to each other in all formations. Finally, one evening an announcement was made that the following named cadets had been classified as pilot and would draw cadet uniforms and supplies the following day. Names were read off: *"Quinlan..."* and skipped Redmond. I was heart broken. I thought I had not qualified. However, the next evening they came in with a new list, and my name was on it. It had never occurred to me that when a new group is formed, they use every other name so that all units have a full alphabetical variety. The next day, I drew my equipment and was amazed at how careful they were to be sure you got a proper fit. When getting shoes for example, you had to stand on a small platform while a shoe specialist checked to be sure that you had been fitted properly. When I tried on my new uniform and saw how nice it looked, it made me feel very proud to be a cadet.

After a slow start, which I now realize was due to the giant problems in setting up a new program (including a new base), things were now speeding up. We were advised that we would be transported to Maxwell Field in Montgomery, Alabama for Preflight Training. The next day we were marched to a railroad siding where we had to wait several hours for the train to arrive. This siding was in the middle of a field where there were no facilities. We could sit, stand, or lay down, all in our new uniforms. After the long wait, the train arrived, and we boarded. The coach I was in was almost an antique. It was hot and soon all the windows were open and the soot from the engine blew into the coach and the inside of your collar got so gritty that when you turned your neck the grit scratched like sandpaper.

After we were underway for a time, the toilet overflowed. To keep your feet dry, you kept them on the seat across from you. When the train started up, the water rushed to the rear. When the train slowed down, the water rushed to the front. Fortunately, it was clean water and after a short time some railroad men fixed the problem. The train ride seemed endless. Actually, it lasted about twenty-four hours with frequent stops and time spent on a siding to allow important traffic to go by.

We finally arrived at Maxwell Field for Preflight Training. After our experience at the Classification Center in Nashville with the new temporary buildings still under construction, we were amazed at the beauty of this field. Rather than being housed in wooden barracks, we were assigned six cadets to a room with a private bath in a permanent stuccoed building with a porch. The rooms were spacious and comfortable. We would be at this base for nine weeks. The first four and a half weeks would be spent as underclass, and the last four and a half weeks as upper-class. As underclass, we had no privileges at all. The only time an underclassman was allowed not to be at attention was when he was in his room. He ate at attention, walked the rat line, (the rat line is the outermost six inches of any walk way which must be walked at a pace of one hundred twenty steps per minute.) He got demerits which had to be redeemed by one hour of walking for each demerit over six in one week. The tours could be walked off only during free time. When a cadet became an upperclassman, he was allowed to be off the base from Saturday afternoon until Sunday evening; however, no one could leave the base with any un-walked tours.

Our training consisted of ground school, close order drill, and physical training. I got in such good shape that I could run the Burma Road (three miles of rough terrain, ditches, and sand pits) and around the airfield (about nine miles) in addition to the full day's schedule of other duties without being tired. I should have been in such good shape when I was boxing in school! There were only a few cadets washed out here, mostly for cheating or military discipline. Life at Maxwell was stressful but satisfying. Even though it was hard to believe, we knew we were doing OK because we were tested each day on the matter covered up to date in each subject.

The single exception to this state of well-being for me was the study of Morse Code. We were required, by the end of our nine weeks, to be able to receive code at a speed of 12 words per minute audibly and 8 words per minute visually. For some reason, I could not seem to grasp it. I sat in the class and tried hard to understand. The instructor promised me that if I relaxed, it would come to me. In the last week of class, I just gave up and stopped trying so hard, and all of a sudden, I began to understand everything that was coming across the wires! In one day, I was receiving code at the high speed as required, and the worry was off my shoulders.

After completing our nine weeks of preflight training, we were ready to start flying. This would be received at a primary flight school. My roommates and I were assigned to Southern Aviation School in Camden, South Carolina. This was one of the premier civilian flying schools operating under contract with the government to provide the first phase of flying to Aviation Cadets. We were delighted with the assignment.

As before, we were marched to a railroad siding to wait for the train. Again, it was a wait of several hours before the train came. We had a similar ride to Camden, except there was no water on the floor of the coach. I guess that we were the most unimportant train on the tracks, because we stopped to allow all the other trains to pass by. Again it took twenty-four hours to make a trip of only a few hundred miles to Camden.

When we arrived at Southern Aviation School, we were amazed. This was like a country club compared to anything we had seen before. There was military supervision, but the instructors were civilian. The mess hall was catered by a civilian catering firm and the food was outstanding. Our day now consisted of half a day on the flight line and the other half devoted to ground school, drill and physical training. We were flying the Stearman P.T. (primary trainer), an open cockpit bi-wing plane with a two hundred twenty five horsepower engine. I adapted to the plane and flying quickly and was among the first to solo. We were supposed to get a flight check after 15 hours, another after 30 hours and a final check after 60 hours. I got my 15 hour check and got no other. My instructor, Mr. Nix told me at the end of the course that I had been passed for the course at my 15 hour check. Of course if I had known this earlier, I probably wouldn't have worked so hard. In addition to learning to fly the airplane, we learned aerobatics such as snap rolls, slow rolls, immelmans, chandelles, lazy eights, split S, and other maneuvers. The aerobatics were really fun.

On my last day of flying at primary, I had a ball. I did things that were not allowed. I was just cruising around when I spotted a Buick on a country road with no telephone poles or other obstructions. I decided to have some fun, and chase them for a while. I came up on them from the rear, swooped over them and down in front. Then I came at them from the side, crossing behind them. Next I crossed in front of them. Then for the finale, I got in front and came at them head on. I was right down on the road, about three feet off the pavement. The Buick swerved to a stop and the two men in it dove for the ditch. Now I had to scram because they might get my number and I would be in serious trouble. I'm sure I scared hell out of the two men, but back then was a lot of fun.

A little later, I noticed a small building built on stilts in the center of a large field. As I turned to look, I discovered that it was a school house because the front door opened and the kids came tumbling out. I dove for the front door and the kids still inside the school were pushing to get out and the kids outside on the steps seeing the plane coming at them were pushing to get back in. The kids in the middle were squirting off the sides of the steps since there were no railings. I realize that these incidents were fool hardy, dangerous and mean, but at that time they were only fun.

In conversations with my instructor, Mr. Nix, we had talked about our cadet life. He knew I had a girlfriend in Camden, that her name was Charlotte Lindler, and that she lived on a plantation named Ingleside a few miles outside of Camden. One day while flying with Mr. Nix, he asked me where Charlotte's home was. I showed him although I had no idea why he wanted to know. We buzzed the house a few times to get the attention of all the people out on the veranda. There was a vast expanse of lawn in front of the veranda with plenty of room for flying and showing off. Mr. Nix shook the joy stick to indicate that he was flying the plane. We made a pass in front of the veranda about two or three feet off the ground and right in front of the veranda he popped the stick forward. The wheels hit the ground and we bounced about fifty feet into the air. I was totally surprised as I didn't know what was happening. We sure impressed Charlotte and her family! Mr. Nix laughed all the way back to the field, but Charlotte was irate. All she could think of was our being killed.

One of the stupid things we did was to stuff our bunks with pillows to subvert the bed check, climb the fence and be picked up by our girlfriends. If we had been caught there was the possibility that we could be washed out. This did not happen often, but I guess the temptation was too great to resist. So far this was like being in school. The war was a passing thought; we were having a good time.

Our time at Southern Aviation School passed too quickly. In addition to the fun of flying, the girls of Camden (who were quite beautiful) always knew when we would be free to come to town and were always ready to meet us.

Almost before I knew it, we were ready to move on to Basic Flying School. We were assigned to take our instruction at Cochran Field, Macon, Georgia. We would again be moved by train, but this time we would get the train at the railroad station in Camden. Since my group had many friends in Camden, we decided to take a taxi to town rather than take the school bus. We knew what time the train was scheduled to depart, but based on our prior experience, we did not believe the train would leave on time. While we were saying our goodbyes, someone suggested that we check and see if the train had even come in yet. We walked down to the station and were amazed to see the train actually leaving. We had to run down the tracks to catch the train. Fortunately for us it had not yet picked up speed and we caught it. The cadets who had already boarded the train were cheering us on. We would have been in serious trouble if we had missed the train.

Our time at Southern Aviation School, while very pleasant and a lot of fun, was nerve wracking too because of the wash out rate. Sixty percent (60%) of the cadets washed out leaving only 40% of the Cadets to go on to Basic Flying School at Cochran Field, Macon, Georgia.

I later found out that the reason for the high wash out rate was because there were limited facilities for training pilots. The army was selecting only those who showed a natural ability and flair for flying. No matter how good you were, or how well you seemed to be progressing in flying, you were always fearful of being washed out. The Wash Out Ride was referred to as the "Maytag Messerschmitt" by cadets.

One of the significant things about the washing out of a cadet was the suddenness of the occurrence. When a cadet was washed out, it almost always was as a result of flying deficiencies. When a cadet had failed a check ride, he would be so notified and instructed to return to his barracks. He was to pack up his belongings and report to some headquarters (I don't know where or what this was). When the class of cadets returned from the flight line that day, the only evidence of the washed out cadet was his empty bed. All evidence of his having been there in the barracks had disappeared. No matter how close or what good buddies you had been with him, it was unlikely that you would ever see him again. The sudden and complete separation of washed out cadets from those cadets continuing in the program, prevented the newly washed out cadets from expressing their frustration and bitterness to the other cadets and degrading morale.

The abrupt separation of close friends was traumatic, but the pressure under which we lived did not permit time for grief. Your thoughts were: "It was too bad, but better him than me." Ranks were closed and life went on. The wash-out situation continued throughout the cadet program until that euphoric day when you received your wings.

Meanwhile, we were preparing for another all-night train ride in an antique coach. After the trip, we arrived at Cochran Field, Macon, Georgia for Basic Flight Training. We were in for a big change in lifestyle from that which we enjoyed at Southern Aviation

School. At Southern Aviation School, while military discipline was maintained, life was much more relaxed. Military discipline at Cochran Field was strictly enforced and fell on us like a ton of bricks. We could live with this, but the food was the worst I ever experienced in the military. If, as occasionally happened, there **was** a good meal, a request to the server for seconds brought the reply, "They ain't no mo'." How we missed the great meals at Southern Aviation School!

After my flying experience in Primary, having been passed for the course without a final check ride, I thought I was a hot pilot, and really did not try as hard as I should have. After three or four hours of instruction, my instructor (an RAF pilot) took me aside to tell me that at first he had high hopes for me, but after reviewing my performance, I had just not developed. He said he wanted another opinion and he was going to put me up for a check ride (wash ride). A wash ride is usually a formality consisting of a ten minute ride around the traffic pattern and goodbye. My wash ride lasted three hours.

When we landed, the check rider, an American Captain, said, (first words) "I'm not satisfied." I nearly died. Then he continued that he was not satisfied that I should have been put up for a check ride and he was going to give me another one. Bad weather held up my second ride for a week. I was a nervous wreck waiting. After my second ride (which lasted another three hours), the check rider said that I had passed, and he would keep me as his student. He was an excellent instructor, but it seemed to me that every ride was a check ride as I was his only student. All his other flying consisted of check rides. After three or four instructional rides with him, he assigned me to another RAF pilot named Pilot Officer Hacker.

Things went smoothly until near the end of the course, when bulletin board postings were made of cadet names, their check rider, and time and date of their final check. Day after day my name did not appear. I was very concerned because I had not had a check ride after being assigned to Hacker. I was reluctant to ask

16

why but I finally approached Hacker and asked why I was not being scheduled for a final check. He looked at me kind of surprised, and said, "Didn't I tell you? The captain passed you for the course when he assigned you to me." I then remembered the captain saying to me when he reassigned me, "Whether or not you are the best cadet on the field, you have to stay out of trouble, because you will not get another chance."

In Basic Flying School we were flying the BT-13, known to the cadets as the Vultee Vibrator. This name was given to it because it was manufactured by the Vultee Company, and it vibrated extravagantly from the powerful engine. The features we were taught included cross country flights, formation flying, aerobatics, and our introduction to night flying. This airplane had an engine that was twice as powerful as the one in the Stearman PT-17. It also had a variable pitch propeller and flaps which helped reduce the take off run and the landing speed. It also had numerous engine controls not available on the Stearman.

A humorous incident occurred to one of the cadets during an Instructional Flight. The BT-13 airplane required the pilot to use 10 degrees of flap for takeoff. This shortened the takeoff run and made the airplane airborne sooner. The flaps were not mechanically powered. It was required that the cadet pilot manually crank them down before takeoff. The effort to crank them down required the pilot cadet to lean down to his left and turn the crank handle. After takeoff, when the airplane is safely airborne, the cadet was then required to reverse the process and crank the flaps up. The motion required by the cadet was fully visible to the instructor flying in the rear seat of the plane. This cadet took off without flaps and after a long takeoff run, was airborne and realized that he had taken off without flaps. Thinking he could fool the instructor, he leaned down and pretended to crank up the flaps. The instructor never acknowledged this and continued the flight.

After landing, both the instructor and the cadet dismounted the airplane and the instructor was speaking to the cadet and told him

17

he was going to asses him 20 stars as punishment (each star represented a 25 cent fine). The cadet acknowledged this and the instructor, an RAF Irishman, about 40-odd years old, asked him if he knew why he was getting the stars. The cadet replied "No Sir." The instructor then advised him that he received the first 10 stars for taking off without flaps. The cadet acknowledged this. The instructor continued, and asked "Do you know why you're getting the second 10 stars?" The cadet replied "No Sir." The instructor replied "You got the second 10 stars for thinking you could fuck an old duck like me and get away with it."

My nine weeks in basic were accomplished with no major upsets after the check ride episode, except for the following cross country experience:

I was scheduled to make a solo cross country flight from Macon, Georgia to Jasper, Florida and return. This was about four hundred miles round trip. It was a beautiful day and I was ticking off my check points when I had the misfortune to see Valdosta, Georgia, way off to my right. The town was laid out almost identically to Jasper. The highways, railroads and rivers were all in the same place. I could not understand how I could have gotten so far off course. It never dawned on me that there was a substantial difference in the size of the towns. Finally, I realized my mistake and tried to correct it by laying out a new course to Jasper. I got lost and to find out where I was, I had to buzz a town to read the sign on the railroad station. Fortunately, this town had a very wide main street with no obstructions. I went down Main Street between the buildings and scared all the good citizens nearly to death. This time not for fun—even though it was! I located myself and flew to Jasper. When I called in my arrival to control, he asked me how much fuel I had left. I was in a glide and my gauges read half full. Control said OK, just buzz the field and go on back. When I leveled out, my fuel gauges read one quarter full. I leaned out my fuel mixture to the point that my engine was almost to the stalling point. I did not get even six inches off course on the return flight. When I landed at Cochran Field, my fuel gauges read empty.

The next day when I reported to the flight line, the ground crew chief was waiting for me. He asked if I was the one flying that plane. I said yes. He said: "You had one quart of gas in each tank. That plane holds one hundred twenty gallons of gas and I put one hundred nineteen and one half gallons in it. You couldn't have gone around if you had missed your landing." We both laughed when he said, "All's well that ends well."

We were ready to move on to Advanced Flying School. The class was getting noticeably smaller as we lost another 60% of the cadets. That means that of the cadets who started with us, only 24% were left.

As we approached the end of our Basic Training, all cadets were offered an opportunity to express their preference for single or multi-engine training. I opted for multi-engine. It was my opinion that most, if not all, cadets got what they had requested. I, with those who had been selected for multi-engine training, moved on to the Advanced Flying School at Moody Field in Valdosta, Georgia.

When we arrived at Moody Field, we were very surprised at our reception. We were treated as cadets who were expected to graduate. We were treated with courtesy and respect every where except on the flight line. On the flight line we were treated like the dummies we were. A much higher level of performance was expected from us than was previously.

For the unwary cadet who, while flying, allowed an instructor to approach close to him without wiggling his wings to signify that he saw him, there was little respect. A formation of all cadets would be held at which a recitation of the offence committed by the unlucky cadet would be read. The offending cadet would be called forward to stand alone at attention during the reading. Then the cadet would be presented with the penalty for the offense.

For the first offense, the cadet was presented with a black arm band signifying that he was a casualty to be considered dead for a period of one week. During this period, the cadet would be shunned at all times except when in his barracks or flying.

For the second offense, the offending cadet was presented with a dumb bell painted yellow with dumb written all over it and worn on a cord around the neck hanging on his chest. This dumbbell was so large that it interfered with ordinary arm motion.

For the third offense, the cadet was presented with the horse blinders. The horse blinders were a real horse blinder cut down to fit a man's head. These were of such a size that the person wearing them could see only straight ahead. When a cadet had been so unobservant that he had received all three awards, he was indeed a very funny sight. Everyone felt sorry for him but he looked so ridiculous, that it was hard to conceal a snicker.

Off the flight line, the cadets were almost treated as officers. The cadet mess was nearly the equal of any officer's club. The food and service was extraordinary. The theme at Moody was "An act of Congress makes you an officer and a gentleman; start practicing.

The strain of washing out was practically behind us. We were expected to graduate. Only a few failed to graduate. I knew none of them and have no idea why they were eliminated. Of the cadets who started training to become pilots, less than one in four completed the course and graduated.

Our flying training at Moody was done in the AT-10 and the AT-9. Both are twin engine planes. Instruction was centered on instrument flying and formation flying. Most of my training was in the AT-10 but we were required to get some time in the AT-9. The AT-9 had a reputation of being a very tricky plane on landing. I don't know how many hours I had in the AT-9 before soloing it and I was getting upset with the delay. I could not see anything wrong with my handling of the plane. I had had no problems at all with the plane on landing, and could not understand the complaints of other cadets on its landing characteristics. Finally my instructor said, "Well I guess you are not going to get into trouble on landing. I wanted to make sure you could get out of trouble, but it appears you are not going to get into trouble, so go ahead and take it up." When I went up without him, that plane did everything it was ever accused of. I had my hands full, but when the flight was over I had mastered that plane.

There were still some RAF instructors on the field. I guess this was the remainder of reverse lend lease. My instructor was an American. There were dual runways in each direction and the RAF pilots (being British) thought they had the right of way at all times, particularly when a cadet is involved. I often did not agree and frequently an RAF pilot had to abort a landing and go around because I would not yield my right of way. They would get my name and order me to give myself ten stars (each star cost twenty five cents). My instructor thought this was funny and asked me if I was trying to run all the limeys off the field. My stars supported the beer bust after the course was completed.

Time went on smoothly in Advanced at Moody Field, except you were never free of the fear that something would happen to cause you to be washed out. However, nothing did happen and on May 28, 1943, I graduated. I was commissioned a Second Lieutenant and was awarded my wings. My parents came down for the graduation as did many of the other cadet's parents. I'm sure they were proud of me. I certainly was!

I could tell they were worried when I showed them my orders. I was ordered to the Combat Crew School at Hendricks Field, Sebring, Florida for training as an aircraft commander and subsequent assignment to a combat crew. I knew my parents were hoping I would become an instructor. I did not tell them that I had been offered the assignment as an instructor, but I turned it down. I wanted to be flying bombers as an active part of the war.

At Sebring, we were taught the B-17 (Flying Fortress) from nose to tail. We spent half of each day flying and the other half alternating days in ground school or working on the line with the mechanics. This was excellent training because it made us totally familiar with the B-17. Part of our training included a cross country flight of at least ten hours. I was fortunate to get a trip to my home city, Buffalo, where the bomber created quite a stir. I was able to take my father through the plane in the early hours of the morning before I left to go back to Sebring.

On completion of the course I was designated an Aircraft Commander and ordered to Pyote Air Base, Texas. There was no time space between schools and training assignments. Three days travel time was allowed to transfer from Sebring, Florida to West Texas. As a matter of fact, I had no leave from the date of my call to active duty till my return from combat two years later. I had no time to gloat over my becoming an Air Craft Commander. The pressure was on to get all the training possible in the short time allowed. (I guess they were anxious to get me into combat quickly to shorten the war!)

Accidents seemed to happen all too frequently and often with disastrous results. On occasion however, a near accident will occur that strains credulity. These accidents are those that are the direct result of a pilot or crew member just not paying attention. These are described by crew members as "having one's head up and locked."

One such accident took place at Pyote during our stay there. The ground altitude at Pyote is approximately 2,500 feet above sea level and since the traffic pattern was to be flown at an altitude of 1,000 feet above ground, the altimeter reading should be 3,500 feet. One night, one of the crews wanting to land entered the traffic pattern—but at an altimeter reading of 2,500 feet. The pilot had misread the altimeter and was actually flying at an altitude of zero feet. The desert was so flat and devoid of obstructions that the wheels which had been lowered actually hit the ground and bounced the plane into the air.

The pilot, realizing what had happened, retracted the wheels and started to climb. I don't know what disciplinary action may have been taken against the pilot, but the indicated altitude for the traffic pattern was raised to 4,000 feet to eliminate the possible confusion caused by the similarity of numbers on the altimeter.

Phase training is divided into three parts. The first would take place at Pyote, Texas and second and third would be received at Alexandria, Louisiana.

Was I surprised on arrival at Pyote! The base had been properly nicknamed "Rattle Snake Bomber Base." It was located in the depths of the west Texas desert. The nearest town was about twenty miles distant and since few of the men had any private transportation, the only recreational facility was the Officer's Club or the Non Com Club on the base. The Non Com Club was a nice club and was completed in final form. Officers were not welcomed in the Non Com Club. What passed for the Officer's Club was temporary and very austere. It was the conversion of half of the officer's mess hall into a club. I was told that a new officer's club was under construction and sure enough it was! I learned that the club under construction was replacing one that had burned down. It was nearing completion. It appeared that it would open about the time I and the crew I was assembling would finish our training. We were flying our last training mission at night and as we circled the field, we observed a huge fire on the base. It was the new Officer's Club burning to the ground. There would be no club for recreation yet.

The first phase training involved the assembly of my crew, acquainting them with the B-17 (none of them had ever been close to one before) and getting to know one another. We had to learn each other's duties and to be able to rely on each other. Our lives would depend on our being able to function as a crew.

23

James J. "Reddo" Redmond, Jr.

I was assigned a co-pilot, Lt. Williamson; a bombardier, Lt. Chang; two waist gunners, Sgt Vinson and Sgt Ward; the engineer, Sgt. Creech; and Sgt. Bogle, Radio Operator. As I said before, none of these men had ever been inside a B-17. They reported to me immediately after graduation from the school of their specialty. It was my responsibility to teach and train these men into a crew. Lts. Williamson and Chang were needed to fill a requirement someplace else, and were withdrawn from the crew. At this point, I had to rely on temporary substitutes until we entered second phase training. I had the right to refuse to accept any potential crew member, but did not exercise this right until we were in second phase. At this time, Sgt. Ward had been accepted into the cadet program and left the crew. In securing the replacement for Sgt. Ward, it was necessary to reject several potential crew members because they did not meld into my fledgling crew. When Sgt. Beyer came up for consideration, he fit in immediately.

Our training, in addition to getting to know one another and learning to work as a crew, centered on bombing and air to ground gunnery. One of the prospective members of the crew complained of airsickness, but with a few trips to the flight surgeon and some counseling he overcame this problem. I was delighted when Sgt. Bogle reported that he no longer needed to carry a can with him on flights! Our second and third phase training would take place at the air base at Alexandria, Louisiana.

An incident occurred during the earlier days of phase training at Pyote. Although it seemed to be unfortunate at first, it helped meld the crew into a unit. We were flying every day and after each flight, the crew walked together back to flight operations. During this walk, we would discuss the flight, what went wrong and what went right. It was during these discussions that we were able to sort out problems before they became serious. On this particular day, the crew did not walk together, but took off immediately after leaving the plane. The ground crew chief called to tell me that some one had gotten sick in the plane. I assured him that this would be taken care of. I called the crew back to the plane. At first they all denied any knowledge of any one getting sick. I had

24

inspected the plane from front to back and knew that it was clean when we took off, and also that some one had gotten sick during the flight. I dismissed the officers because none of them had been in the waist section of the plane. Then I invited the crew to sit under the wing of the plane while we found out who got sick. I sat under the other wing to give them privacy to talk about it. After a little while, they all volunteered to clean it up. I asked if they all got sick. Of course they all said no. Then several crew members offered to clean up the mess, but they denied being responsible.

I thought I was losing this battle because by now an hour and a half had passed. I told the men that if it took until tomorrow morning we would sit under that plane until we knew who got sick. Then out of the blue, one of the men spoke up and said he got sick. I said," OK, clean it up." He asked if that was all and I said yes. Then another member of the crew asked if he could help. I said "Sure, all I wanted was for them to acknowledge the problem and admit it." The guilty man said if he had understood, he would have spoken up immediately. He was afraid I would have him grounded. I explained to them that when something happens which may bring trouble, I wanted to know immediately and I wanted to know the facts, good or bad. I wanted to know the truth. I explained that we were a crew - that we were all on the same side. I explained that if any of the facts needed to be shaded, I would do the shading. I told them I needed the plain unvarnished truth so I couldn't be blindsided. I explained that I was their airplane commander and I would back them all the way. This incident went a long way toward cementing the men into a crew. It paid dividends throughout our career as a combat crew because whenever a problem arose, I could handle it. I knew the facts accurately, not as they might be embellished by another party.

A perfect example of how this understanding with my crew worked occurred at Syracuse N.Y., on our way overseas to England. We were expected to post a guard on our plane during the hours of darkness. I arranged a schedule and relied on the men to adhere to it. I was gone from the base over night and when I returned the next morning the whole crew sought me out to report that the plane had not been guarded during a good part of the night. Then they told me the underlying facts. The plane had been guarded continuously well past midnight when a change of the guard was to take place. The relief guard due in at midnight could not find the plane in the blacked out field. He went into the operations office to report that he could not find the plane, and requested transportation to find it. He was refused. He made another attempt to find the plane but was unsuccessful. The guard who was to be relieved at midnight stayed with the plane until 3 AM when he left the plane. No sooner had I received this report from my crew, when I was summoned to the operations office where I could expect them to give me hell. I expected them to carry on about the plane being unguarded and the danger of sabotage. They would plan to report this to the Commanding Officer etc., etc. I was absolutely correct. They carried on about all of these things. However, since I was in possession of the real facts I was able to suggest that the matter be reported to the commanding officer, and the operations officer could explain why my crew man was refused transportation when he had reported that he was unable to find the airplane in the dark. The scenario now changed and the operations officer saw no reason to bring this to the attention of the Commanding Officer. I had no desire to see the Commanding Officer either and was happy to drop the matter while I was ahead. There were a number of other examples of how this honesty in the crew saved us from trouble. On several occasions, I was told about occurrences that never developed into problems.

Before we had to report at the air base in Alexandria, we were given a six day delay in route. This allowed about three days at home and was the only time off I, or any of the crew, had before going overseas to England and combat. At Alexandria, I received the rest of the candidates for my crew. These included the navigator, Marty Strom, the bombardier, Tony Wagner, the ball turret operator, Sam Bell and the Tail Gunner, Vernon (Shorty) Palmer. There were several candidates for the remaining waist gunner position. These were rejected since they did not seem to fit in with the crew members already selected. The successful candidate was Wilbert Beyer, who was about thirty five years of age. He was far and away the oldest crew member. One of the determining factors in his selection was (I thought) that he would be a stabilizing factor on a young crew. Although this proved to be not accurate, he became a valuable crew member and remained with the crew through our thirty four combat missions. I had a temporary co-pilot until we arrived in England at our air base where Frank Cavanaugh joined the crew as co-pilot.

The second and third phases at Alexandria were combined to speed up our arrival in combat. The training here really intensified. The emphasis was on formation flying, air to air gunnery, and bombing. It was during these exercises that the crew really became a crew. Each one knew his job and his responsibilities, and could perform without a hitch. The pressure was on because this was the only time we would have to perfect our performance. Our next experience would be in combat over Germany. By then I thought I had assembled the finest crew possible, and I was ready to go to war with them.

However, with the intensification came tragedy. There were several fatal crashes in a two-week period, although I only saw one of them. The one I saw took place at night when another B-17 caught fire. I have no idea what caused the fire, but when I first saw it, the plane was completely enveloped in flames. It was flying at about the same altitude as I, and I followed keeping in radio contact with the Alexandria Tower. The whole occurrence was over in a few minutes, when the plane nosed over and crashed. I advised the tower of the location of the crash and went on to complete our exercises.

We were expecting our orders to go overseas when Wilbert Beyer, my 35 year-old waist gunner came to me and said he wanted to get off the crew. I had a difficult time controlling my temper. I could not understand how he could go all through training as a crew member and now at the end of our training, when he was a valuable member of the crew, he wanted off. I thought he was just afraid of going into combat and was wasting our time.  I thought he had no consideration of the void his departure would leave.  He did not seem to have good reasons as to why he wanted to leave the crew.  When I was about to give up on him, I found out the real reason he wanted to leave the crew.  He told me that he wanted out because he thought when he got to a combat area he would be grounded and not be allowed to be air crew because of his age.  I assured him that no one would ground or remove any member of my crew after we had trained together for so long.  He reacted with enthusiasm and this solved the only problem he had, now he was anxious to remain on the crew.  I was never concerned about his age or the possibility of his being grounded.  I felt that these problems had already been faced when he was classified as eligible for air combat duty, and that any candidate referred to me was cleared by higher headquarters.

In early November 1943, we got orders transferring our crew to Kearney, Nebraska for overseas staging and to take possession of our new B-17.  What a thrill this was!  *Our own brand new B-17!* This was the first time I was even close to a brand new B-17. Everything was clean and shiny.  All the B-17s I had flown up to this time had thousands of hours on them.  We did not know that we would not get to keep it after we got to the E.T.O. (European Theatre of Operations).  This plane had only four hours flight time on its log.  This was the time required to flight test it and fly it from the Boeing Plant in Seattle to Kearney.  After being assigned this airplane, we flew an acceptance check to determine that everything was in good order and working properly.  Our code name for the trip was "Damsel D Dog."  After several days in Kearney completing the necessary formalities, we were cleared to leave.

The first leg of our trip was to Syracuse, N.Y. We arrived in Syracuse in the late afternoon.  After taking care of the necessary paper work and being sure that the well-being of the enlisted men of my crew had been taken care of, I caught the next train for Buffalo.  I was only able to visit with the family until midnight when I caught a train back to Syracuse.

During our flight from Kearney to Syracuse, the cabin heater was found to be defective and on landing we notified the ground crew. They checked and found a defective part. They promised to replace the part. We were to depart the next day, and on arriving at the flight line, we found that the part had not been replaced. I started to raise hell with the crew chief who said he did not have that part and would have to go to the Rome Air depot to get one. I told him to get his ass in a jeep and go get the part—that I was not going to leave until the heater was repaired. He reluctantly agreed. The next day the plane was ready to go, but the weather closed in again. It cleared in two days, but then my ball turret operator Sam Bell came down with the flu.

Sam spent eight or ten days in the hospital. The authorities wanted me to leave him and go on saying that he could catch up. I refused to leave him, contending that he might never locate us. This would destroy the crew that we had spent so much time and energy in forming. Keeping the crew intact was imperative.

They finally agreed and we waited for him to recover. We spent about ten days in Syracuse and had a ball! Syracuse is a sizeable town and had a university full of girls. There were practically no men since there was no military installation near by. All good things come to an end, and any way we were on our way to fight a war.

Our next leg took us to Presque Isle, Maine. The weather now was very poor and we were held up in Presque Isle for several days. One day the weather looked as though it would be good all the way to Goose Bay, Labrador, so we loaded up and flew in very nice weather to Goose Bay. When we got there, the tower announced that the field was closed. They were experiencing a blizzard. We questioned them because there was only one cloud in the sky and it was located right over the field. The tower said that cloud had been stationery for an hour and there was no indication that it was about to move. The field was closed and did not expect to open anytime soon. We circled the field and its cloud and returned to Presque Isle. A few days later we successfully made the trip to Goose Bay. We had gotten up early to fly to Goose Bay, and had horsed around the rest of the day, not resting, but enjoying this northern country.

About dinner time I was notified that we were expected to fly out that night. I did not say anything, but I decided I was not going to fly the north Atlantic without a good night's rest. I knew that we would have to take off before midnight so that the navigator could use the stars for navigation. I followed all the directives, went out to the plane, got everything ready in case we had to go, then we sat back and wasted time. There were a great number of planes going tonight, and the tanker trucks were busy fueling up the planes. I did not flag any of the tankers and waited until all the tankers had returned to the motor pool. It was now approaching midnight when I called the tower and complained that I had not been able to get gassed up. I said that the trucks were ignoring me. The tower operator blew his top, but said that he would have a tanker come back out. A tanker came back out and gassed us up. We re-checked everything, wasting more time then called the tower told him that we were ready, and asked for taxi instructions, just as innocently as though it was two hours earlier. The tower operator had another fit, then cooled down a bit and told me that it was too late to go, to shut the plane down and go back to the BOQ (Bachelor Officer's Quarters). Before we could leave the plane it was necessary to put wing covers on the wings. It was so cold (minus 40 degrees) and the wind was so strong, that it took until three AM to get them on. The weather got bad again and we were stuck for about ten more days. It was OK with us.

We were the only transient crew on the base at Goose Bay and became acquainted with some of the permanent party. They were friendly and grateful for the opportunity to talk to people who were newly arrived from the States. We were told that there was a Hudson's Bay Trading Post only 35 or 40 miles distant from the Air Base. We did not know how long we would be in Goose Bay, but with the help of our new friends, we secured the use of a truck to take us to the Trading Post. The local weather was pretty good and we took our B-17 and inspected the road to the Trading Post.

It looked good so we made arrangements to go to the Post the next morning with the intention of buying some expensive furs and mailing them back home as dirty laundry. Before we could start for the Trading Post, we were notified that the weather would be good that night for the ocean crossing, and we should be ready to go. This was the end of our plans to visit the Trading Post.

We were now rested and ready. After dinner, we had a weather briefing. Marty Strom, the navigator, got his maps, checked his sextant, and got ready for a long night of celestial navigation. Wes Creech and Sam Bell, the engineers, re-checked everything mechanical. Lloyd Bogle made a number of radio checks to be certain that his radios were functioning properly. This time we were ready substantially before midnight.

We took off and had an uneventful trip most of the night. It gave us a thrill when Marty Strom came on the interphone to announce that we were just passing the point of no return. The only person working during the crossing was Marty Strom. The whole responsibility for a safe crossing rested on his shoulders. If he made even a very minor error, it could be curtains for all of us.

Just before sunrise, I noticed what I thought was a ship on fire. It didn't seem to be too far away and I called every one's attention to it. We started to fly toward it, but we didn't seem to be getting any closer. I asked Strom to estimate its position, and we would send an SOS for them. The flames seemed to be leaping hundreds of feet in the air. I had Lloyd Bogle, the Radio Operator, tune in his radio to be ready to send the SOS. About this time, Strom came on the intercom and said don't send anything, that is Venus, the morning star. We continued on course and quite rapidly the fire disappeared and was replaced by the star. It is impossible to describe this spectacle. You have to see it to believe it!

We had been warned that the Germans were broadcasting a radio beam from the Cherbourg Peninsula to attract American bombers over their territory so they could have the opportunity to shoot them down. The frequency on which they broadcast was almost the same as one the British used to help guide the Americans to England. We intercepted both beams and could understand why a number of American bombers had used the counterfeit beam and found their way into trouble.

It was a great relief when we sighted land, even though we had never had the slightest concern about a successful crossing. Marty Strom had done a masterful job of navigating. After a flight of over 3000 miles, most of it at night, we crossed the Irish coast on a direct line for our destination, Nuts Corners Air Field, near Belfast. Marty Strom was exhausted from the trip, as much from the strain as from the actual work. He called on the intercom and asked me if I thought I could find the field. I said sure, but I found that Ireland does not look anything like the USA. In a matter of seconds, I was lost. I called Strom and told him, but now he didn't know where we were either. I decided to use the radio to find out where Nuts Corners was. I reached the Nuts Corners Tower and they advised me that they were the field with three runways near a lake. At this moment I could see three air fields each with three runways and each near a lake. I decided to land at one of them and find out where we really were. I started on a final approach to one of the fields and they were giving us red lights indicating that they did not want us to land. I was ignoring the signal and was coming in for a landing when they came on the radio and told me that Nuts Corners was straight ahead over the next hill. I pulled up, went over the hill and landed.

When we left Goose Bay, the temperature was 40 below zero. Here, in Nuts Corner, the temperature was in the 40's above. It seemed like the tropics, so we took off our heavy clothing. We gradually put the heavy clothing back on because it was so damp that the cold went right through the clothing. Marty Strom was exhausted from the trip. He was the only one who did not get any rest. When all the necessary had been taken care of and our first day in the E T O was drawing to a close, McLott (my temporary co-pilot) and I decided to go and see Belfast. We put Strom to bed and covered him with a great number of damp blankets. He slept until the next morning, but it took another day before he had recovered his usual energy.

We had changed all our American dollars into British pounds, shillings and pence. We were ready and anxious to visit Belfast. We had not been briefed on the customs and practices of the citizens nor given any idea of what to expect. Yesterday we were in America; today we were in Belfast. We had no idea of the value of anything and I am sure we were taken a number of times. The bus driver had assured us that the bus terminated in the downtown section of Belfast.

When we left the bus, we were indeed in downtown Belfast, however, darkness had fallen and we were treated to a number of experiences that we had not been cautioned about. These were concerned with our introduction to the blackout and the impossibility for a newly arrived American to find anything or any place in such total darkness. We were also exposed to the substitutions the British had made for the shortages of gasoline, or as the British call it, petrol. We also found that even though the British speak English it is not always the same as that spoken by the Americans. Rather than interrupt the progression of our odyssey, our experiences in Belfast are described in detail in the section titled *"Ancillaries, Vignettes and Combat Statistics."*

While at Goose Bay, we had the opportunity to stock up on things we suspected would be in short supply in England. We had heard stories that candy was scarce in England so we bought about 15 cases of different kinds of candy bars. We had not heard any stories about canned fruit juices, but it seemed likely that fruit juice might be scarce and highly desired. We bought about 20 cases of different kinds of fruit juices. The candy was not heavy and did not take up much space, so transporting this would not be much of a problem. The fruit juice, however, was another story. It was heavy and took up a lot of space. We had not expected to have our plane taken away from us at Nuts Corners, but it was taken and sent to a modification center to be prepared for combat. We were flown to Glasgow Scotland, and from there we went by train, with several transfers to a replacement base near London. Each time we had to change trains it was necessary for us to physically transfer our fruit juice and candy from baggage car to baggage car (there was no station help available). When we took time to check on our candy and fruit juice, we found that the candy was all gone. The gunners had eaten all of it. Their only explanation was that they were hungry. The fruit juice was intact and we hoarded it until we reached our permanent station at Polebrook. Then we had the surprise of our lives. Every morning at breakfast there was a large container of fruit juice with no restrictions on how much you drank. We consumed our fruit juice in the barracks in the evenings.

We spent a week or ten days at the replacement depot near London. The officers attended ground school to prepare us for combat and the gunners were given a training course of their own. While we were at the replacement depot, there was a bombing raid on London. This raid took place at night and we sat on a low stone fence and watched the raid. It was really exciting. We could see the search lights looking for the bombers, and on one occasion we saw the light focus on a bomber and the anti aircraft flak shoot it down in flames. We would see the flash of the exploding bombs and a few seconds later we would hear the explosion. This was the only time I ever saw a bombing from the ground, but it gave me a good idea how terrifying it must be to be right in the target area. The next day, I was offered my choice of assignment to one of two groups that needed replacements. I noted that my friend, Bud Ritzema, pilot of another crew, with whom I had been close friends all through combat training had been assigned to one of these two groups. I selected the one that Bud Ritzema had gone to. This was the 351st Bomb Group located at Polebrook. We were assigned to the 509th Squadron.

We were transported by truck to the 351st Bomb Group. Our travels were now over for the time. This is where we will spend our foreseeable future. Officers are quartered separately from the enlisted men on the crew. After I had satisfied myself that my gunners had been taken care of properly, I saw to the officer's quarters. There was not much choice. We were assigned to a barracks which had four empty bunks. We were told by the other officers in the barracks that the crew occupying the bunks had been shot down a few days ago. We moved our belongings in and discovered that what served as a mattress were three pads, called biscuits. These were filled with horse hair and were hard as bricks. All the other crews in the barracks had real mattresses. We found out that as soon as a crew was shot down, their mattresses were grabbed by some one who was sleeping on biscuits. We had to wait until another crew was shot down and we could get our real mattresses. As more mattresses came to the base, the biscuits became surplus, and we used them as cushions on the chairs we had around the coke stove.

One night, one of the barracks members having a last cigarette before going to sleep, flicked the butt toward the stove, but it missed the stove and landed on one of the biscuits and smoldered. Some time later, a commotion woke me up. I saw that all the lights were on, but the smoke was so dense I could not see the other side of the barracks. I could see that some persons were fighting the fire, so I figured that if it got serious, they would get me up. I pulled the blankets up over my head and went back to sleep. When I got up the next morning, the burned biscuit had been thrown outside but the smell from its burning stunk up the barracks for a month.

The Base was laid out beautifully. The combat crews' quarters, the Combat Officer's club, the NCO (Non commissioned officers) club, Squadron Headquarters and the flight line were all grouped closely together. The ground echelon was located a short distance away. The food service at this base was superb. The club officer won several awards for having the best in the Eighth Air Force. Not only was the food good, it was cheap. The procedure for charging the officers was to have each of them sign a sheet every time they had a meal. At the end of the month, a bill was rendered. Never once did my bill exceed the 21.00 per month food allowance we received. The high quality of the food service was explained when I found out that the head chef at M G M Studios in Hollywood had been flying as a gunner on a combat crew when Clark Gable recognized him. Gable brought this to the attention of headquarters and he was taken off flying status and put in charge of food service in the combat officers club.

We even had ice cream which was made by a British ice cream plant. The Americans provided the ingredients and the British manufactured it. Then for some reason, they refused to make ice cream any more. We were without ice cream. Of course the combat crews complained bitterly. One afternoon, the club officer approached me and asked if he made ice cream, would I take it up to 30,000 feet to freeze it. I said certainly, and the next day we had ice cream. Later the USA bought the ice cream plant from the owners, and hired them back to make the ice cream. For some reason, as part of the arrangements, no ice cream could be served to any English, (there was no ice cream available in all of England) but the Eighth Air Force had ice cream again. If we had a guest for dinner in the officer's club, it was necessary for you to request a second serving and carry it to your guest.

We were at the 351st for several weeks before we were assigned to fly any combat. During this time, we flew practice missions and became acclimated to the base procedures. After we had become familiar with the routine of life at the 351st Bomb Group and had proved ourselves to be a proficient combat crew, we would be assigned to a B-17. We expected to be assigned to the brand new B-17 G which we had flown from America, but this was not to be. We were assigned to a B-17 F.

The principle difference between a G model and an F model was the addition of a chin turret with two 50 cal. machine guns and electronic supercharger controls. We were initially disappointed, but after meeting the ground crew chief, Ed Kurek and his men, we fell in love with "My Princess." She was battle scarred and a veteran of a number of combat missions. We were told that the pilot who had been assigned to her previously and who had named her had been shot down while flying a different plane. We decided not to change her name and we flew her on a large number of missions. She was a faithful plane, and with the superb maintenance of Chief Kurek and his crew, helped us establish a record of never having aborted a mission.

We held the experienced crews in awe. They had "seen the elephant" and knew what combat was. We were just waiting around for our turn. The experienced crews would tell us about combat, but we didn't know whether or not to believe them.

The non-flying officers were in awe of the combat veterans and we knew it. There was a separate officer's club for the ground people. The flying officers referred to the ground officers as "Paddle Feet." Since the paddle feet did not see combat and had every reason to expect to survive the war, they did not drink as much as the combat officers. Their club usually had booze leftover long after the combat officer's club quota had been consumed. The combat officers, faced with the uncertainty of life, were often quite rambunctious. When the mood would hit us, we might get a little buzz on and walk down to the ground officer's club to drink their booze and maybe start a little trouble. When we entered the club, most of the paddle feet would leave immediately. We would have a drink at the bar, then turn from the bar and look over whatever officers were left. Pick out one or two and go over and scare hell out of them. We never touched one of them, but the possibility was always there. We were being immature and cruel, but the pressures under which we lived—ranging from total peace to abject terror—sometimes produced unusual results.

An incident occurred one night at the ground officers club that I thought was funny. A late snack was served at both officers clubs. They were comparable, but different. For example, the ground officers club regularly served hot cocoa whereas the combat officers club did not. I have always liked hot cocoa for a late snack, particularly with toast with lots of butter. In order to make toast, it was necessary to stoke up the coal stoves which had been banked for the night. I had been in the habit of making toast in this manner for some time. The mess sergeant would be livid because he would have to rebank the fire. We had had words about this, but I continued to make my toast. The mess sergeant had told the club officer about this and he had obviously told the sergeant to get him the next time it happened. On this night, I happened to run into the catholic chaplain who was a regular guy. I told him about making toast and he was all for it. It never occurred to him that there was anything wrong with it. The chaplain and I were busy working on the stove when the door burst open and the club officer and his sergeant charged in. The club officer hollered get away from that f—stove you sons of bitches. Then he saw the chaplain, and he started on the sergeant about "why didn't you tell me the chaplain was involved"...The chaplain didn't know what was going on, he was asking "Are we doing something wrong?" I told him no, the club officer was all upset about something else. We finished making our toast, but that was the last time I tried to make toast.

Then there were the parties.

The officer's club held their party on the last Saturday of the month and the NCO club held their party on the mid Saturday. This assumed that no mission was scheduled for the following Sunday. In that event, the party would be rescheduled for the next Saturday. The same ladies (I think) came to both parties. Whenever we met a girl, we would remind her about the Polebrook party. At about 7 PM on the appointed night about 12 big covered trucks would pick up all the ladies on the appointed corner and bring them to the club. We had lots of booze because the club officer had been saving up for the party. The G.I. band would provide music for dancing until midnight.

I think everybody had a good time at these parties and when the party was over all 12 trucks would line up in front of the club to take the ladies back home. One or possibly two trucks would get a full complement of ladies who did not connect, or whose morals would not permit them missing the truck. The empty trucks went back to the motor pool and the ladies who stayed, went to bed. The next morning there was very poor attendance at breakfast but all other meals were well attended. The ladies would not miss a meal while on the base because our menu was superior, and the British were subsisting on a Spartan diet. It was considered bad taste to keep a lady on the base past the third day. As time passed and the war got more organized, no lady was allowed on the base before 5 PM. This regulation was designed to eliminate the presence of the ladies on the base for extended periods. It was effective to a certain extent, but some combat crew men simply kept their ladies in the barracks and brought their meals to them until 5 pm, when the ladies would be welcome in the officer's club and the NCO club.

One occasion that I remember well, involved my co-pilot, Frank Cavanaugh. He got drunk one night and his wanderings took him into the main kitchen where there were a number of frozen turkeys laid out to thaw. They were to be the entrée at dinner the next day. Frank thought it would be a good idea to bring a turkey back to the barracks and cook it on our coke stove. This turkey was of huge size and still had the head and feet attached. We convinced Frank that we could not cook the turkey and he agreed to return the turkey to the kitchen. By the time he got back to the kitchen, the turkey had been found to be missing and the M.P.'s (Military Police) had been called. The situation was reported to the squadron's commanding officer, Col. Le Doux. The colonel brought Frank up on charges and wanted him to sign a document stating that he was caught stealing a turkey from the mess hall. Frank refused to sign until the document was altered to say that he was caught returning the turkey. His penalty was a fine of $75.00 and confinement to quarters for 30 days. He could leave his barracks only for meals and flying.

During the month of Frank's incarceration, we all had a 48-hour pass which left Frank all alone in the barracks. He looked pitiful as we were leaving. We felt so sorry for him all alone in the barracks for 48 hours that when we returned to the base, we brought a girl for him and a bottle of liquor. She was really beautiful - one of the best looking girls I had seen in England. She lived in our barracks for about five days. Since no party had taken place recently, she was not noticed. When we were on a mission, she would be on the flight line sweating us out. The guys in the other barracks were jealous but could not tempt her to leave us and move to their barracks. She might have been with us until the end of the war except that one evening in the queue for dinner she was standing in front of me and the base commander, Col. Romig, was standing behind me. I don't think the Col. even knew she was on the base until she saw him and recognizing his rank started to flirt with him. Word came down from headquarters that it was time for her to leave so we put her on the bus to town. We were sorry to see her leave, but we had a war to fight. The fact that women were allowed on the base was not an official position. Rather it was just not officially observed. Possibly the fact that a combat crew man might be at the party tonight and not be alive tomorrow affected the protocol.

On those days when there was no combat mission and the weather was passable, we would fly a practice mission. This was just like a combat mission, except that we did not carry bombs or guns. The emphasis was on formation flying. This was so important. It could mean the difference between life and death. The German fighters would pass up a group flying good formation to attack one flying a ragged formation. If they attacked anyway, and you were flying good formation, the formation protected you. Some days we would fly to a bombing range called Scares Rock and drop 100 pound practice bombs to give the bombardier some practice. On still other days, we would go to a wrecked B-17, and the whole crew would practice getting out of the plane supposing that it had been a crash landing and fire was imminent. We also practiced bailing out of the same wreck. Since the parachute was not worn during combat (it was too bulky), the practice trained you to not forget the parachute and to know the exit you were to use. There would be no time for errors.

Combat crews were required to fly a tour consisting of twenty-five missions. I will go into detail about combat missions later. Twenty-five missions were considered to be the maximum number that a combat crew man could stand before cracking up. In order to help the crews attain this goal, each combat crew was given a ten day leave at about the midway point of their tour. This leave would be spent at a resort area in England with the costs paid by the government. We selected the resort town of Southport, which was located on the coast of the Irish Sea.

Southport was a real resort before the war, but now the amusement facilities had been removed. We all had a very restful time with no concern of having to fly any missions. It was early spring and the weather was beautiful, so some of the crew and I decided to go swimming. I have never been in such cold water in my life. It was not refreshing, it was freezing! There were a considerable number of young ladies in town and we managed to meet our quota. One such encounter that I remember well went somewhat like this:

My whole crew was in the pub of one of the better hotels and I had gone to the loo (toilet). When I got back to the crew, they had a table full of very pretty ladies. There was an older woman who seemed to be in charge of them and after a few drinks the woman said that they were going to a dance and if we wished to accompany them, we were welcome. We all thought the woman was a madam and the ladies were her girls. We were wrong. The girls were domestics and the woman was taking them out for a night. As we were walking to the dance, my lady and I kept falling back from the group trying to ditch them. The woman was very watchful and would drop back and bring us up to the group. It was very difficult to give her the slip because it did not get dark until almost midnight. At the dance, we had a riot! We even learned to do a dance called 'The Hokey Pokey.' My lady was a domestic at a very plush residence. We dated several times during our stay in Southport as did the other crew members. After our leave was over, we were supposed to be ready to go back into combat but we were ready to go back to Southport!

When we were selected to go on our mid tour leave (known by the combat crews as Flak Leave), we did not think that we really needed one. We felt that we were just as combat ready as we were when we first started flying missions. During our time at

Southport, away from the stress of having to fly combat, we could see that our nerves and general physical deportment had deteriorated and that the time away from combat was necessary. When our leave time expired, we were like a new crew, except that we were experienced. We returned to combat with an enthusiasm that had been missing only ten days ago.

We were fortunate that we had been selected for the Flak Leave when we were because the ferocity of the German fighter attacks and the intensity of the flak barrages, if anything, had increased. We understood that we might not have been able to perform if we had not been taken off combat for a ten day rest.

With the uncertainty of life, we grabbed at what fun was available and interspersed with combat missions; our path seemed to seek out wild times and wild ladies.

We had heard such wild stories about a pub called 'The Robin Hood' in Leeds that we could not believe them. We had to go and see for ourselves. We arranged a forty-eight hour pass and were set to go to Leeds the next day, but we got scheduled for a mission. The mission takes priority, so Leeds and the Robin Hood would have to wait. We were up before 2 A M and prepared for the mission. After breakfast, briefing and get ready time we were in the plane ready for take off at 7:30 AM. Then, as so often happens in England, the weather began to deteriorate. We sat in the plane while take off was postponed one half hour at a time until the mission was cancelled at 10:30. Now that there was no mission, our pass was valid again.

It was necessary to take a bus to Peterborough where we would take a train to Leeds. The last bus in the morning left the base just before the club opened for lunch. We had no alternative but to skip lunch. In war time England, restaurants were open only during lunch and dinner periods. When we got into Peterborough, lunch period was over and the restaurants were closed, but the bar in the railroad station was open and serving. We drank until the train left at 5:30 PM. We boarded the train and got into Leeds

42

just after the restaurants had closed. By this time, food was no longer a priority. I split from the crew to see if I could get a room at the Grand Hotel. The Grand and some other hotels had no vacancy so I gave this up as a bad job and joined my crew at The Robin Hood Pub. The Pub was terribly crowded but the crew had obtained a large table. However, with the ladies they had collected, there was no available seat for me. An RAF pilot was seated at a nearby table and when he left his chair for some reason I grabbed the chair. After a drunken argument, we decided that since he was sitting in the chair before I arrived, it must be his.

As I was standing at the table talking with my crew, I made the acquaintance of a tiny blonde. After a while, it became obvious that there would be no place to sit and she suggested that we visit another pub in the neighborhood. I agreed and we left.

At some time during the evening, after my lady and I had agreed that we would spend the night together, it was necessary for us to have some place to stay. I had already checked several hotels and found no vacancy. However, my lady being a native, had other sources. We repaired to the taxi cab station where my lady called her landlady. The conversation as I recall it from my drunken condition went something as follows: "Oh yes mum, he's very nice. Oh yes mum, he's a lovely Yank. Oh yes mum, we'll be no trouble. We'll be ever so quiet, you won't even know we are there. Oh thank you mum. We'll be there directly. Yes we are coming by taxi."

After we arrived and I was duly inspected by the landlady, we began the climb to our room. We were on the fourth floor and as we passed the third floor, my lady wanted to visit a friend of hers who lived on the third floor. We found her friend in her room and lo and behold, she was in the sack with a Canadian. We visited for a few minutes (it was like visiting in a hospital). We sat on straight back chairs and conversed with her friend and the Canadian as they reclined in bed. Although the Canadian was friendly or as friendly as could be expected, I suggested that we allow them to

43

get to sleep or whatever it was they wanted to do. We left and climbed the last flight of stairs to my lady's room. For the night it would be our room.

Since I had eaten nothing since breakfast at 2:00 AM, and had been drinking since noon, I was now thoroughly drunk. After we reached our room and settled in, I discovered that I was unable to perform (a brand new experience for me). As bad as this was, I now got sick. I'm sure this capped a terrific evening for my lady. We were on the fourth floor and the bath room was on the third floor. I staggered down the hall and down the stairs to the bathroom, all while I was stark naked. I don't know if anyone saw me or not. In my condition, it didn't even enter my mind. The next morning I was the victim of the worst hangover I have ever had.

I wanted to get out into the fresh air, but as I was going down the front steps, the land lady appeared and called to me, "You haven't had your breakfast yet, please come in and have some tea, beans and toast." It hurt to talk, but I convinced her that I didn't want any breakfast. Then she said "You haven't washed yet." I told her that I had and she replied, "But you couldn't have, for I didn't draw water for you." I gave up and went back into the house and was directed into a large parlour. The landlady brought a basin and a pitcher of warm water. My lady of the previous night (having freshened up) came into the parlour and she and the landlady sat and watched as I washed my hands and face. When I had washed to everyone's satisfaction, my raging hangover and I departed.

When I left the house, I had no idea of where I was. I selected a route that looked as though it would take me to the down town section. I had no idea of where any of my crew was, so I could not look for them. My walk took a couple of hours and did bring me to the rail road station. Although my head was clearing, I still felt terrible so I decided to take the first train back to Polebrook. By the time I got back to the base, I was feeling a little better but I immediately knew that something was wrong. The atmosphere over the field was morbid. I found out that the group had flown the exact same mission that we had been briefed for the previous day with no changes. The crew that had replaced us in the formation had been shot down. This was their first mission. The group had lost four bombers to a fighter attack and most of the returning planes had suffered severe damage. The number of wounded crew men was high. Some of the crews speculated as to whether the Germans had advance awareness of the mission. My crew returned the next day with lurid tales of the fun they had had in Leeds at the Robin Hood Pub but the tragedy of the mission we had missed spread a cloud of gloom over everyone. This again made us realize that this was war and how terrible war is. It made the fun we had seem very unimportant.

Relationship with members of other crews sometimes became moderately close to the extent that, as a regular practice, you would dine or drink together. When crew in such a relationship got shot down, the others would unconsciously wait for them to appear. After a few minutes, the realization that they would no longer be a member of the party is recognized and new associations are made. Very little grieving takes place. It is war and life goes on. In this regard, I mentioned previously that when we were being assigned to a combat group, I elected to come to the 351st because my best friend, Bud Ritzema, had been assigned there. I did not suspect that he would be shot down on his first mission.

We had been very close during training and had been roommates for months before we came to England. I had no expectation that his time with the 351st Bomb Group would be so short. On his first scheduled mission to Achmer, Germany on February 21, 1944, he experienced a runaway prop on take off, and being unable to take off, ran off the end of the runway. He was a good pilot and was able to bring the plane to a safe stop. There was no fire or explosion and none of the crew was injured. The next day February 22, 1944, my friend, Lt. Ritzema flew on a mission to Magdeburg, Germany, and as he passed the Ruhr Valley he was shot down by a flak barrage. Because of our long close friendship, Ritz was missed longer than most.

On June 6, 1944, "D" Day, Joe Berardi, another Airplane Commander and I flew our 30th mission. This would complete our tour. It was customary that on the last mission of a tour, the pilot was entitled to buzz the field. The number of crews completing a tour was so few that it was unusual for two crews to compete their tour on the same day. Because of this, unusual occurrence Berardi and I planned to fly a formation buzz job. This would be the first one flown. When we found that this was "D" Day we felt that there was too much going on for us to play. After we landed, we thought we had completed our tour, were finished with combat and would be returned to the States. We were then notified that in view of the invasion taking place and the uncertainty of success there were no tour limits and we were expected to continue to fly combat.

We were again faced with the necessity of flying more missions after we had completed our tour. This created a real mental hazard. Everyone who found themselves in the position of having to fly more missions after completing his tour was worried that his luck had run out, and that he would get shot down. I really didn't think I would get shot down, but I wasn't very sure of it.

That evening, both Berardi and I were pissed off over having completed our tour and then being told that we would be expected to continue flying combat. We went to the officer's club and proceeded to get pretty drunk. After we had a pretty good buzz, we decided to visit the Ground Grippers (Paddle foot) Club and perhaps make some mischief. After another drink or two, at the ground officer's club, we spotted the base commander and the deputy base commander. We decided to make them aware of how displeased we were. We proceeded to become quite obnoxious. I don't know what Berardi said to his colonel, but I bearded my colonel about how many missions he had flown. He said he had flown 25. Then I would tell him that I had flown 30, without an abort, and I was still flying and I was pissed off. I can remember him being very agreeable and listening to my complaints and trying to placate me.

After we had finished with the brass, we left the club and spotted the base commander's jeep (Colonel Romig's). It had previously been announced that there was concern that the Germans would drop parachutists onto bomber and fighter bases to disrupt air support for the invasion. Combat crew enlisted men who had completed their tour were placed on guard duty to counter any German action. Berardi and I decided to take the colonel's jeep, inspect the guards, and make sure there were no Germans on the base. Berardi was driving and I had all I could do to keep from being thrown from the jeep. We careened from one guard to another. We would demand the password, inquire about German infiltrators and caution the guards to be on the alert. The poor guards, all enlisted men, didn't know whether to shit or go blind with two drunken flying officers checking their station. As we approached the last one that we inspected, we could not get any satisfaction. All this guard could do was laugh. He knew me and all he could do was say "it's Lt. Redmond," then he'd go into gales of laughter.

I was so drunk that I could not identify him. I suspected that he might be a member of my crew. In conversations much later with Sam Bell, my ball turret gunner, I found out he was the guard in question. It was too dark and I was too drunk.

After completing the guard inspection detail, we decided that we should check the main runway to make sure that no German parachutists had landed on it. We made several runs in both directions in the pitch black night at full speed and determined that there were none. We were now beginning to sober up and realized that we had better return the colonel's jeep before it was discovered to be missing. We headed back and decided to take a

47

short cut through a large mud puddle. Before we could get through it, we found ourselves stuck axel deep in the mud. The jeep was plastered with mud and generally a mess. Since we couldn't move the jeep, we left it there and walked back to our barracks. I don't believe the colonel ever really knew how we provided security for the base that night!

During the period from June 6, 1944 and June 19, 1944 I had flown three more missions and on June 20,1944 I was scheduled for and flew a mission to Hamburg, Germany. We got back to the base in time for a late lunch. There was supposed to be another mission that afternoon to the invasion coast. I did not feel tired, and since this would be a short mission, and it was rumored that the new tour limit would be 35 missions. I volunteered to go. At lunch, fatigue set in and I was sorry that I had volunteered. While I was regretting having volunteered, an announcement was made that anyone who had 30 missions on June 6, 1944 ("D" Day) was finished. I had a total of 34 missions. It was great to know you have finished your tour and have done what you set out to do but it was a let down. Something is missing from life. Your goals have been reached and where do you go from here? Actually, while you were fearful of each mission, you miss the excitement and anticipation.

I had completed my tour, and this signaled the breakup of my crew, "Reddo's Raiders." The various members of the crew had completed slightly different numbers of missions due to being grounded occasionally for a minor physical ailment or having to fill in on another crew. Some of the members of my crew who still had a mission or two to complete their tour would fill in on other crews.

I had no duties to perform now that I had completed my tour, and my life changed completely. I was no longer a combat crew member. I no longer belonged to that select group of men who were straining to complete their tour. I was accorded the highest respect and was envied for having completed my tour but I was no longer one of them. It was sort of boring hanging around the base so I made several visits to London, but it was strange. It was not the same. The pressure and strain that I lived under for the past many months was gone and I had the feeling of nostalgia for the fearful days of combat.

After a few weeks my orders were cut transferring me to Glasgow Scotland, where I waited another week or so for a convoy to be assembled to take me back to America. When the convoy was ready for loading, I and those combat veterans who were being returned to the States, were taken out to the ship in a small boat. We waited for another day before the convoy was ready to sail. I found that we had been assigned to a former luxury liner. The total complement of passengers was a few hundred. On the ship's voyage to England it carried about ten thousand soldiers. We had deluxe quarters on this ship, a first class cabin with private bath and shower. I found life on board ship materially different from life in England. For example, I had the first white bread since I left the States. In England, our ration of candy was two candy bars per week. I was not a big candy eater States side, but when it was rationed, it became very precious. On board the ship, it was not possible to buy a candy bar, the candy was sold only by the box. As soon as the scarcity was gone, the desire for the candy disappeared. There was not very much to do on the ship and the high points of the day were the meals. They were delicious. The food we had been served since leaving Polebrook was not very good.

In talking with some of the ship's crew, I found out that we were following the Northern Route, which would be quite cold even though it was summer and would take longer to get to America, but it was safer from attack by submarines. After we were underway for several days, we encountered a bad storm. Our convoy consisted of about 40 ships and the captains had a hard time keeping the convoy from breaking up. The storm produced waves over 40 feet high so that the nose of the ship would plow under the wave and the stern of the ship would come completely out of the water. The propeller would spin until the governor controlled it. Meal time was hilarious. The dishes would slide all

49

over the table, but a barrier on the edge of the table top kept them from tumbling off. Frequently when attempting to place a spoon full of food into your mouth, with a lurch of the ship, your hand and spoon would miss your face and mouth completely. I spent one whole afternoon sitting on the stern of our ship expecting to see the two ships behind us collide. They came perilously close frequently but they never hit. The storm was exciting and I enjoyed it until I learned that the convoy was making no headway, but only trying to keep the convoy intact.

The trip to the United States took a little over two weeks and what a welcome sight the Statue of Liberty was! It gave me a thrill to be an American. Our ship was anchored in the middle of the harbor less than a hundred yards from shore. I could see the traffic on the streets and people walking. It was hard to believe that this was really America, and those people were really Americans. America was still out of reach. We lined the railings of the ship yearning to get ashore. It took three or four hours before space was cleared for our ship to dock. We were greeted by a military band which welcomed us back. I guess this was because we were early returns from combat. There were very few before us. From the dock, we were bussed to Ft. Dix where we were processed and released on a 30 day leave. I caught a sleeper to Buffalo, and arrived unannounced to my parent's home that next morning. Nobody was up yet, but my parents got up shortly, because my dog, Pete, did not recognize me at first and raised a storm until he finally recognized me.

I waited in the sun parlor for them to get up and I felt sort of funny as to how to act. It had been over two years since I left their home to become an Aviation Cadet and a lot had happened during those years to the kid who left and the combat aged man who returned. Things were a bit stilted at first, but this feeling quickly vanished, as we hugged each other. My parents made me feel so welcome that it was hard to realize that I had been gone so long. The surprise of my return was shaded by my telling them in letters that I had completed my tour, so they had some expectation of my return.

I had a 30 day leave; my first leave since my call to active duty two years ago; and I intended to enjoy it. I guess I was a hero, although I didn't know it Everybody seemed to know me, and people I didn't know would stop me on the street to talk to me. This adulation was heady, but a little goes a long way. I guess I could not fault them because I was one of the first to return from combat and the people were hungry to meet and talk to someone who had been there. Even Curtiss Wright, the airplane manufacturer, called and invited me to tour their plant. It was fun being a celebrity, but towards the end of my leave it got a little tiresome. After my leave of 30 days, I was ready to go back to flying and my military life.

On the expiration of my leave, I was ordered to Atlantic City for re-classification. This was a procedure in which it was determined to what specialty the returned combat veterans would be assigned. We were afforded the opportunity to request any assignment you wanted. Your request would be taken into consideration, but their determination was final. Most of the pilots were assigned and orders cut within 4 days. The great bulk of assignments were to the training command as instructors. I did not want this assignment, and I had avoided it when it was offered to me when I had first gotten my wings.

When four days had passed and I had not received an assignment, I suspected that something was up. I started to have interviews with progressively higher ranking officers. After a few days I discovered that I was being considered for assignment as a liaison officer in one of the military hospitals. I was interested and got to the point of having my choice of a hospital in Cleveland, Ohio, or Carlyle, Pennsylvania. I had selected Cleveland. My last interview was with a full colonel and our discussion centered around flying. He probed about how much I liked to fly and about the duties in the hospital. He finally smiled and said that he did not want to put a pilot who really enjoys flying into a job that will only afford four hours flying a month to qualify for flight pay. He assigned me to the Ferrying Command, which was my original request.

I had been in Atlantic City for 12 or 14 days when I received my orders to report to the Ferrying Command in Nashville, Tennessee for further assignment. This ended a real vacation of 12 or 14 days. It was August - the height of the tourist season - and the city was loaded with thousands of young ladies. There were less than 800 returned Air Corps veterans and practically no other men. It seemed as though the Board Walk was loaded with finalists for the Miss America Pageant. It is surprising how selective a person becomes when the odds are so great.

Going back to Nashville was almost like returning to the beginning, even though I did not see the old classification center. I was there only three or four days when I was ordered to Great Falls, Montana. I had a pleasant surprise in Nashville. My cousin Evelyn and her husband John Cleary were there. We spent a few pleasant evenings together. John was a Navy Lieutenant waiting for a barge to be built that he was to command. My assignment to Great Falls was just what I wanted. I was moving planes all over the country. For example, I would go to the Boeing Factory in Seattle, pick up a brand new B-17 right off the assembly line and deliver it where ever it was wanted. Sometimes Great Falls, sometimes Atlanta, and sometimes Kearney, Nebraska. At other times I would be required to fly a B-25 bomber to Fairbanks Alaska for delivery to the Russians. At the time the Russians were our allies (or were supposed to be). However, most of the American pilots delivering these planes took an intense dislike to the Russian pilots. They were exceedingly arrogant and acted as though we owed them these planes. Of course there was no opportunity to converse with them because of the disparity of languages, but we could read their body language very clearly.

There were other planes to be moved and other destinations, but the trips to Alaska were my favorite. The scenery was so beautiful that it defies description. I was free to land for lunch at places like Skagway, White Horse, and other places in the Yukon that I used to read about when I was a kid. The only drawback was the urgency of delivery of the planes which stopped us from loitering along the way.

In the fall of 1944, the Japanese started sending balloon bombs over the Pacific Ocean to the Northwest United States. The primary purpose of these bombs was to start forest fires in the heavily wooded northwest. There was not too much concern about civilian casualties since the balloons carried a limited amount of explosives. The primary load was incendiaries. Actually, the only casualties were a family of six who were killed in Montana. These balloons were a startling development, since no one ever thought that a balloon could be sent with the jet stream from Japan to the United States. As a matter of fact, America did not even know of the existence of the jet stream. Our base was alerted, and I was sent on several search missions to look for the balloons. I never found one. The existence of the balloons was never made known to the public since we did not want the Japanese to know that any of their balloons reached the United States. We were afraid that if they ever found out that any of their balloons were reaching the United States, they might arm the balloons with poison or germs. In all, the Japanese released 9,000 balloons and 1,000 reached the United States.

An interesting thing happened on one of my many trips to Seattle, when an Army nurse wanted a ride to Great Falls. I had plenty of space since there was only me and the co-pilot. She was very pretty so I agreed to take her to Great Falls. There was lots of room in the waist of the plane and this was when I became a member of the yet to be formed "Mile High Club." Unfortunately, I could never brag about this, or as a matter of fact, even admit to it.

On one of my trips to Seattle, I met a young lady named Betty Jean Hewitt employed at Boeing. We became close friends and after few months she told me that she was going to return to her home in Sioux City, Iowa. I convinced her to stop over in Great Falls. She did and we were married.

*James J. "Reddo" Redmond, Jr.*

I had always been a very good instrument pilot, and I enjoyed instrument flying because it was a challenge. When it was announced that they needed an Instrument flying instructor, I thought I might like to try it. I applied for and got the position. I was happy doing this, but I missed the freedom and variety of delivering planes all over the country. While I was ferrying planes, I had the opportunity to fly almost every plane the Air Corps had. Although I was not a fighter pilot, I did fly a P-51 once. There was no one available to fly it that was qualified. I volunteered, and after a cockpit check, I took off and delivered it. Flying that Mustang was a sensation.

It was required that all instructors take a refresher course, and I had been sending the instructors in my flight as their turn came, never thinking that at some time I would be the only one left to go. That day came in late July 1945. I went to Bryan Texas, and was about half way through the course, when the atomic bomb was dropped. The next morning, we were assembled in an auditorium and were made to select whether we wanted to remain in the post war military, subject to probable overseas assignment or wanted immediate release from the military. No one could leave the room until they had made a choice. All through my military career, I had planned to remain in the Air Corps but when they insisted on a selection right now, I decided that if this was the way they were going to act, I would get out. I returned to Great Falls and remained there until I was separated to the reserves.

About six months later, I received notice from the Air Corps that I should report to Ft. Dix for consideration for a regular Army Air Corps Commission. I reported to Ft. Dix and underwent a number of tests and interviews. After each one, you would be advised if you had passed and who would be your next interview. I passed all the tests and interviews and was advised that I would be notified. I was later notified that I was accepted and placed on a list from which available openings would be filled. At this time, the army was in a reduction of forces, and very few were accepted for a regular army commission. I had not placed high enough, and I was never called.

I continued in the active reserve until 1958, attending annual two week active duty tours and monthly weekend duties until my job responsibilities became too demanding, and I was transferred into the inactive reserves. The highest rank I attained was major.

# SECTION TWO

## THE COMBAT STORY - DECEMBER 1943 TO JULY 1944

## FORWARD

The statistics and descriptions of combat presented herein were obtained from several sources. Those of numerical form were obtained primarily from reference books in the Miami, Ft. Lauderdale, and Hollywood, Fl. Libraries. Additional material was obtained through the facilities of the Florida Library System and their nation wide search facilities. Much information was obtained from the many books authored by Roger A. Freeman, Kit Carter and Robert Mueller.

The descriptions of combat missions were provided primarily by diaries maintained by me as each mission was flown. These were supplemented by conversations and correspondence with surviving crew members, specifically, Lloyd W. Bogle, Radio Operator, Sam Bell, Ball Turret Operator, and Tony Wagner, Bombardier. These crew members also contributed to the section "Ancillaries and Vignettes."

Unfortunately, when I decided to write my long overdue memories, six of our combat crew members were deceased. They could not contribute to this effort as they had so valiantly during our combat tour.

Our crew was known as "Reddo's Raiders" and was, in my opinion, the finest crew assembled in World War II. Each member was an expert in his field and contributed fully to our performance. Our remarkable record of surviving thirty four missions and never aborting one was unique in that very few crews could make that claim.

Expertise in their military specialty was extremely important, but even more important was their ability to function as a team—and that is what made a good crew, superior. In combat, each crew member could attend to his own responsibilities, confident that all other crew members were performing at one hundred percent.

I hope this writing will serve as testimonial to the loyalty and performance of this terrific crew, the strong bonds and trust in each other without which we could not have survived our tour of combat.

The crew of "Reddo's Raiders" was singular in that from the very first time they met each other there was an instant sense of recognition that they would meld into a crew. The assembly of our crew was begun in Pyote, Texas and continued in Alexandria, LA. We trained one month in Pyote, and two months in Alexandria, after which we were ready to go to war.

In late 1943, we flew to England, and joined the Eighth Air Force. As we moved into combat, it was with the confidence and security that I had as perfect a crew as possible. We could rely on each other without reservation. Because of crew cohesion, we completed thirty four missions without loss of life or an abort. We were the sum of our hard work and determination.

The narrative of this commentary in may seem to center on my impressions and reactions, and overshadow the part played by my crew. This is due to the fact that I was not moved to record this bit of history until many of my crew had passed on, and therefore they could not contribute. As I said before, the crew of "Reddo's Raiders" was in my opinion, the finest ever assembled. Without them and their steadfast loyalty to me and each other, it is quite possible that we might never have completed our tour and survived the war. Their loyalty and performance helped win the war.

## MEMBERS OF THE CREW OF "REDDO'S RAIDERS"

**FRANK CAVANAUGH, OUR CO-PILOT.** Frank's home was near Boston in a suburb called Brookline. He had a famous father also named Frank who was a World War One hero. He was memorialized in the movie "The Iron Major," starring Pat O'Brien. This movie was produced in the 1930's. After the war, Frank Sr. became a nationally famous football coach. Our co-pilot, Frank, acknowledged the relationship but never tried to trade on it.

As a co-pilot, Frank was superb. He would sit in the right seat, all six feet four of him and direct the fire of the gunners, calling out the direction of attack, conducting oxygen checks, and generally supervising the crew. His value to the crew was demonstrated by comparison with other co-pilots who flew with us on those few occasions when Frank could not. During most of our tour, Frank was disdainful of protective gear and did his job unprotected. As we approached the end of our tour, Frank brought additional pieces of protective gear to wear. One day, I asked him why he was now wearing more and more protection. He replied that he never expected to complete his tour, so he sat up bold and brave to do a good job. Now that it looked as though he had a chance of completing his tour, he was determined that if he got shot, it was not going to be his fault. On his second to last mission, all you could see of him were his eyes peering out from a pile of armor and still doing his job. I told him that all that protection was fine, but he had better be prepared to fly without all that protection because I was going to let him fly his last mission as Aircraft Commander. He did, and so finished his tour.

**MARTY STROM, OUR NAVIGATOR.** Marty was from Enumclaw, Washington. He was a tall slender blond, very handsome. He was about 22 or 23 years old. His position in the plane was at a table below and forward of the cockpit, but to the rear of the bombardier's position in the nose. He had a fifty caliber machine gun on each side of the plane which he was expected to man when we were under attack. It is necessary for him to move from one side of the plane to the other, depending on which side was being attacked. He was also expected to know where we were at all times. He was a star navigator as evidenced by the masterful job he did guiding us across 3000 miles of the North Atlantic, most of it at night. When we made landfall in Ireland, we were right point perfect on target. Numerous planes on similar flights got lost and were never heard from again. When returning from a mission, frequently in a crippled condition, Marty would guide us so we could miss most of the flak barrages. The location of the navigator's guns did not provide a good firing angle so that it was unusual for a navigator to actually shoot down an enemy plane. As you will see later in this section on combat missions, Marty was credited with one ME 109, shot down.

**TONY WAGNER, OUR BOMBARDIER.** Tony was from Detroit, Michigan. He was an excellent bombardier, very accurate and very serious. While we were in training in the States, he was credited with several "shacks." A shack is when the bombardier actually hits the target with a bomb or puts the bomb within a circle with a ten foot radius. Tony sat in the very nose of the plane, and while he enjoyed the excellent view required by the operation of the Norden Bombsight, he was totally exposed in the Plexiglas nose of the plane. Tony was very cheerful and happy although very quiet. He did not participate in some of our ribald adventures taking place when on pass, although he enjoyed hearing about them later. Tony seemed to be a little on the bashful side, although I don't know how he could have stayed that way being a member of our crew.

Tony was very popular with the other members of the crew. They knew he was solid and reliable. On one of our missions, (one which all of our crew members will never forget), after Tony had dropped the bombs, or thought he had, the radio operator who is responsible for checking to make sure all the bombs have left the plane, called to report that there was a bomb hung up in the bomb bay. It was Tony's responsibility to get the bomb out of the plane. The bomb was fully armed and was hanging by one connector so it was swinging back and forth with movements of the plane. We could not bring the bomb back to the base because of its potential to explode during landing or any other disturbance. Tony knew the bomb was his responsibility. In order to release the bomb, Tony would have to enter the open bomb bay. He had to first put on his parachute to protect him if he fell out, carry a walk around oxygen bottle and his tools. While so encumbered, he had to get the bomb out. Tony worked on the bomb for ten or fifteen minutes. He was hanging onto the support girders in the bomb bay while suspended over the open bomb bay twenty five thousand feet up. Finally, he announced that the bomb was gone. The whole crew breathed a sigh of relief. No one noticed where the bomb went or if it hit anything. All we knew was that it was over Germany. Tony was the hero of the day.

**LLOYD W. BOGLE, OUR RADIO OPERATOR.** Lloyd was from Hanna, Oklahoma. He sat in the radio room which is located just aft of the bomb bay. There is a door at the entry to the bomb bay and one at the entry to the waist section. When both doors are closed, it makes the radio room much warmer than other sections of the plane. However, being cloistered with both doors closed can make it a little claustrophobic. The radio operator's gun is mounted in the Plexiglas escape hatch in the roof of the radio room. The only area the radio operator can see or protect is the area straight above the plane.

Lloyd was a Cracker Jack radio operator, but he was sometimes a little forgetful. Such as the time he forgot to get the pilot's flimsy for me. The flimsy was a small sheet of rice paper on which were listed all the radio codes for the day. Without the flimsy, I would not be able to contact anyone. It was a very secret document which was to be swallowed if capture was possible. At "start engines," I discovered that Lloyd had not given me the flimsy and when questioned, he said he had forgotten it. I ordered him to go and get it. We were parked a long way from the radio shack; and I did not think he would be able to get it before we had to take off. I had decided that if he did not get back I would go without him. Fortunately, he was able to get someone with a jeep to drive him to the end of the take off runway. I was just starting to run up my engines for take off when Sam Bell called and said "Bogle is here, wait a minute." I retarded the throttles, Lloyd got on board and we took off with the tower operator calling to find out what was wrong. Lloyd never forgot the flimsy again.

Lloyd was a sometime comedian as was evidenced one day when we were undergoing a vicious fighter attack. The radio room was very cloistered and the only outside vision the radio operator had was straight up, where his gun pointed. All the guns were firing, noise was deafening, and the plane was vibrating as though it was about to come apart. Lloyd could not see any of the action and he came on the intercom to announce that since he couldn't see anything he was going to hide under the radio table. Incidents like this - while not exceptional in their re-telling - had a calming effect on the crew. Sometimes even the smallest of things can be monumental.

**JACK VINSON, OUR WAIST GUNNER.** Jack was from Valhalla, South Carolina. He was a quiet type of guy. He usually went along with the crew and was agreeable to whatever they wanted to do. He had a great amount of courage which came to light when the crew told me that he was so terrified in combat that he could not fire his gun. I seriously considered having him grounded but I did not want to take the risk of having him replaced by some one who would not fit in with the crew. I discussed this with the crew and they unanimously decided that they did not want to trade Vinson for an unknown. Pop Beyer, the other waist gunner said that attacks from the 3 o'clock and 9 o'clock positions seldom occurred simultaneously since the enemy fighters would be on a collision course. He maintained that he could handle both guns. Based on this, I kept Vinson on the crew. He flew his full tour even though he was so terrified that he never fired his gun in combat. This situation was kept as a crew secret, and no one else ever knew about it. Jack flew every mission even though he was petrified with fear. While this was stupid and fool hardy, I thought it showed real courage. My decision to keep Vinson on the crew may have been correct or incorrect, but this was war, and difficult decisions had to be made.

**WILBERT (POP) BEYER, OUR WAIST GUNNER.** Pop came from Walnut, South Dakota, and was the oldest member of the crew. At 34 years of age, he was 12 to 14 years older than the rest of the crew. When he was assigned to the crew, I was concerned about his age but I thought he might lend some maturity. I decided to give him a chance and see how he worked out. He soon became a member of the crew fully accepted by the other members. He became a good crew man, but he provided no maturity. He became one of them and while he was and looked 34 years old, he was ready for any nonsense the crew might suggest.

Pop trained with us as a crew member for three months. Pop flew all his missions, completed his tour, and manned both his and Vinson's gun capably.

**SAM BELL, OUR ASSISTANT ENGINEER AND BALL TURRET GUNNER.** Sam was from St. Louis, Missouri. He was a quiet unassuming person, but when he made a statement, you could rely on it being accurate. He was a graduate of Engineering School in addition to gunnery school. While his title was Assistant engineer, he functioned as Co-Engineer. Before a mission, I knew I could rely on Sam having rechecked everything on the plane, regardless of whose responsibility it was. Sam served all his missions flying in that uncomfortable, scary ball turret. Sam knew that the ball was the most dangerous position in the plane, and that the casualty numbers of ball turret operators far exceeded that of any other position in the plane. He never complained or suggested that he fly in a different position. As a matter of fact, when positions were being assigned, Sam volunteered for the ball. The entire crew admired and respected his courage. He was an excellent gunner, receiving credit for enemy planes destroyed.

**WES CREECH, OUR ENGINEER AND TOP TURRET GUNNER.** Wes came from Whiteville, North Carolina. He was an excellent engineer, monitoring the engines and instruments. I gave him lessons on flying so that if anything happened to incapacitate the pilot and co-pilot, he would be able to keep the plane flying. This might make it possible for the plane to make it back to England or to allow the crew to bail out. He was a good student and enjoyed piloting.

**VERNON (SHORTY) PALMER, OUR TAIL GUNNER.** Shorty was from Mellette, South Dakota. He was the youngest man on the crew. He was very outgoing and happy and the most enthusiastic man on the crew. Occasionally, his enthusiasm had to be stepped on. For example, frequently on a mission, after the bombs had been dropped, Shorty would be so relieved and happy that he wanted to sing. This would be OK because singing would not interfere with being alert to watch out for enemy fighters, but Shorty would serenade us on the intercom. This would prevent other members of the crew from calling out fighter attacks. However, one word from me and the entertainment stopped.

**ED KUREK, OUR GROUND CREW CHIEF.** Ed's home was in Pottsville, PA. Ed and his crew tended "My Princess." She was their plane, and they were responsible for all maintenance. Our lives depended on them. They would work twenty-four hours if necessary to provide us with as perfect a plane as possible. They practically lived in a tent erected at the hard stand where "My Princess" was parked so they could have her ready for the next mission. On our return from a mission, the ground crew first checked on the well being of the combat crew, and being satisfied that we were well, they would swarm all over the plane to see what battle damage needed to be repaired, and what mechanical attention needed to be given the engines. Our record of never having aborted a mission is the result of the quality of the work of Chief Kurek's Ground Crew. They were responsible in a large measure for our having survived our combat tour.

In summary, as I have said previously, in my opinion, this was the finest combat crew assembled in the Eighth Air Force in World War II. When we had completed our training and were scheduled to go into combat, I knew I was ready to go to war with them. Their performance in combat proved me right.

# PHOTO SECTION

"My Princess" B-17 Flying Fortress piloted by Reddo Redmond.

Reddo's Raiders

(Back Row, Left to Right): Wesley J. Creech, Engineer, Lloyd W. Bogle, Radio Operator, Wilbert "Pop" Beyer, Waist Gunner, AJ Vinson, Waist Gunner, Samuel M. Bell, Ball Turret Operator, Vernon "Shorty" Palmer, Tail Gunner. (Front Row, Left to Right): Donald McLott, Temporary Co-Pilot, James J. "Reddo" Redmond, Jr., Pilot, Martin L. Strom, Navigator, Anthony Wagner, Bombardier.

This is the BT-13 (Basic Trainer) Plane

Another BT-13 flown for nine weeks at Cochran Field for Basic Training.

This Stearman PT-17. This was flown in Primary Training School
for nine weeks at Southern Aviation School.

This is a Beechcraft AT-10 twin engine trainer flown for nine weeks at Moody
Field, Valdosta Georgia.

The Curtiss AT-9 "Fledgling" aka "Jeep"—Advanced Trainer airplane.

I took this picture from the window of "My Princess" during a combat mission over Germany. The other four planes in the distance are also in my formation and are other B-17s.

Aerial View of the 351st Bomb Group Base at Polebrook, England

| | | | |
|---|---|---|---|
| 509th Squadron Op | 13. Main Hangar | 25. Gym | 37. Motor Pool |
| 2. 509th Breifing Room | 14. Group Gunnery Ofice | 26. Church Army | 38. Parachute Shop |
| 3. 509th Drying Rm | 15. 509th Armament Office | 27. Main Gate | 39. Officers Quarters Ground |
| 4. 509th Orderly/Mail | 16. 510th Armament Office | 28. Enlisted Mens Barracks | 40. Automotive Main Shop |
| 5. Navigation Rm | 17. 508th Armament Office | 29. 509th Supply Room | 29. 509th Supply Room |
| 6. Hospital | 18. Photo Lab | 30. Flak Suits | 42. Flight Crews Barracks |
| 7. Officers Club/Mess | 19. AML Trainer Building | 31. Polebrook Lodge | 43. Guard House Officer of Day |
| 8. Officers BBQ 509t | 20. Link Trainer Building | 32. Aux. Hangar A | 44. Sheet Metal Building |
| 9. Sergeants Club | 21. Spotlight Trainer Building | 33. Aux. Hangar B | 45. Water Tower/ Weatherman |
| 10. Enlisted Men Mess | 22.Cleaning & Laundry Officers | 34. Control Tower | 46. Bomb Site Building |
| 11. PX | 23. Staff Officers Mess | 35. Fire Trucks | 47. 510th Orderly Room |
| 12. Post Office/Barber | 24. Group Headquarters | 36. Welding Shop | 48. 511th Orderly Room |

Our barracks in Polebrook England.

Another shot of our barracks in Polebrook, England.

Our base - Polebrook, England.

Guard House and guards at main gate at Polebrook.

*James J. "Reddo" Redmond, Jr.*

James "Reddo" Redmond, Aircraft Commander, in the cockpit of MY PRINCESS.

Sam Bell, Ball Turret Operator, after a mission on MY PRINCESS.

Wilbert "Pop" Beyer, Waist Gunner, prior to truck ride to Debriefing Room.

Lloyd Bogle, Radio Operator, on the ground, post-mission.
In the background is Tony Wagner (left) and Jack Vinson (right).

Co-Pilot Cavanaugh, on ground after a mission.

Wesley Creech, Engineer (right) and friend, at barracks in Polebrook.

Crew after a mission. Facing the camera, from left to right is Wesley Creech, Engineer, Ed Kurek, Ground Crew Chief and Frank Cavanaugh, Co-Pilot.

Ground Crew Chief, Ed Kurek.

*James J. "Reddo" Redmond, Jr.*

Jerry Viste, (center) another pilot and "Reddo" (right), barracks, Polebrook
England.

James "Reddo" Redmond (front), Pilot and Sam Bell, Ball Turret Operator,
in front of MY PRINCESS.

Our navigator Marty Strom (front row, right) with another crew after a mission on which he substituted for their temporarily grounded navigator. Back row, left end, Joe Berardi, pilot of this crew, and back row right end, Joe Heard, co-pilot.

Our Navigator, Marty Strom, in front of MY PRINCESS.

Our tail gunner, Vernon "Shorty" Palmer in MY PRINCESS.

Tail Gunner, Vernon "Shorty" Palmer in front of his barracks, Polebrook England.

Tail Gunner, Vernon "Shorty" Palmer, on ground after a mission.

My crew, on flak leave. (Left to right): Shorty Palmer, James "Reddo" Redmond, Lloyd Bogle and Jack Vinson.

Another picture of us on flak leave. Back Row, left to right: Lloyd Bogle, Marty Strom, Jack Vinson, and kneeling is Shorty Palmer.

Radio Operator Lloyd Bogle with local boy while on flak leave. We teased him relentlessly that this was his child!

Tail Gunner on flak leave in Southport, England.

Vinson with some local gals in the hamlet of Polebrook.

Tony Wagner in front of MY PRINCESS after a mission.

Marty Strom and wife June, upon graduation from
Navigation School, July 1943.

Tony Wagner, Our Bombardier, 1943.

Tony Wagner, ~ 1997.

Flak as seen from a B-17 of the 351st Bomb Group during a raid on Berlin on March 4, 1944 as seen at www.polebrook.com.

The cockpit of a B-17 Flying Fortress aircraft.

Black Thursday Photographs taken from a position behind the pilots seat through the windshield.  It is believed the pilot shown in the top photo is Col. Budd Peaslee.  Both pictures provided by Col. Gene Carson.

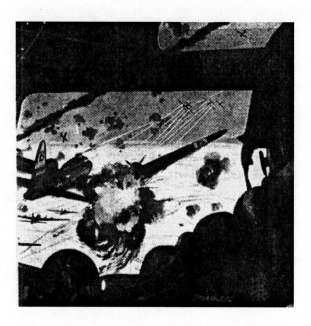

B-17 Damage Photo, USAF Official Photo provided by Col. Gene Carson.

Contrails from a B-17 formation flying overhead; official USAF photo
provided by Col. Gene Carson.

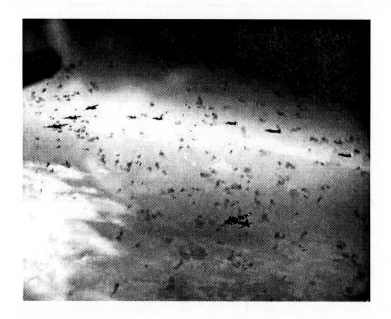

Heavy flak in the air; official USAF photo provided by Col. Gene Carson.

B-17 Damage photo provided by Col. Gene Carson.

*James J. "Reddo" Redmond, Jr.*

Assistant Engineer and Ball Turret Operator, Sam Bell.

Radio Operator, Lloyd Bogle, ~ 2001.

James J. "Reddo" Redmond, Jr.
Pilot of "My Princess" B-17 Bomber
US Army Air Corps 1943-1944

Jim "Reddo" Redmond
~ 2000

*James J. "Reddo" Redmond, Jr.*

Current Pictures of Reddo as he inspects the ball turret operator's space on the B-17 on display at a local air show.

Reddo in the year 2000 as he inspected a B-17 flown into Florida for an airplane show.

Reddo routinely volunteers with the Carling Foundation with first-hand knowledge about the B-17 and World War II when the B-17 is placed on display in the south Florida area.

Reddo wearing his Bomber Jacket—front patch represents
the 509th Squadron of the 351st Bomb Group.

Back of jacket. "My Princess" is the name of my plane. The Triangle J
represents the 351st Bomb Group, and is the insignia on the vertical stabilizer of
all 351st B-17s. To either side of the USAF star in the white spaces, the name of
the crew "Reddo's Raiders" is lettered. Each bomb below the Circle Star
represents a successful mission flown over Germany and Occupied Europe.
There are thirty-four in all.

91

*James J. "Reddo" Redmond, Jr.*

Polebrook Memorial to the 351st Bomb Group at the Airfield in England. Photo taken while attending the Reunion in June 2000. *"IN MEMORY OF THE 351ST BOMBARDMENT GROPU (HEAVY) EIGHTH UNITED STATES ARMY AIR FORCE. 311 GROUP COMBAT BOMBING MISSIONS WERE FLOWN FROM THIS AIRFIRLD OVER OCCUPIED EUROPE BETWEEN 1943–1945. 175 B-17 FLYING FORTRESSES AND THEIR CREWS WERE LOST. 303 ENEMY AIRFCRAFT WERE DESTROYED IN AERIAL COMBAT."*

Photo of Joe Dixie at the 351st Reunion in San Diego June 2001! The remarkable thing about this photo is that on the June 14th, 1944 mission to Paris, I saw Joe Dixie's plane explode. I did not see any of the crew bail out, and assumed that all the members of the crew were killed in the explosion. I can still see that great orange ball of fire as his plane was destroyed. I was more than startled to see him alive and well at the reunion!

The nose of a B-17 flown into southern Florida for an airshow.

The same B-17 with Reddo, John Sullivan (grandson) and three of Jim's great-grandchildren in the spring of 2000.

*James J. "Reddo" Redmond, Jr.*

# THE COMBAT MISSIONS

On subsequent pages are listed the combat missions participated in by "Reddo's Raiders" as members of the Eighth Air Force during World War II.

The missions are listed in chronological order of their happening and the narrative describing the mission was compiled from my diaries kept during the war as supplemented by conversations and correspondence with crew members. Following the heading of each mission narration, is shown the number of heavy bombers of the Eighth Air Force that were lost on that mission. The grand total of heavy bombers and their crews lost in the Air Offensive was 6,533.

As a prelude to our first mission, I want to describe the atmosphere surrounding our crew and the impending mission.

I could feel the tension embracing the crew members, including me. It had been building up for the past few days, ever since we had been notified that we would be flying on this mission. We were facing the unknown and the fear of the unknown. We had observed the loss of planes and crews from missions flown while we were waiting our turn to go. We had no idea of what it would be like. Stories told by experienced crews did not help. We were like babies who are about to have their umbilical cord cut. I thought I might help by speaking to the crew.

It was almost time to board the plane and start engines when I gathered the crew together and asked if there was any one who did not think he was going to complete his tour. No one responded. I then said if there was any one who did not think he was going to complete his tour, I did not want him on my crew. I said that if there was any one who had any doubts about this, I would transfer him to another crew. Again no one spoke. After a short wait for comments, I said, "This crew is going to fly its twenty-five missions and complete its tour, so let's get aboard and see what this is all about." We boarded the plane and went on our first mission.

Actually, I lucked out on this one because I don't know what I would have done if anyone had spoken up. While I was sort of bluffing, it had the desired effect. It made the crew a little belligerent as we went to war.

In order to understand and appreciate the following listing of combat missions, it is necessary to understand what is involved in planning and flying a mission.

The itinerary contemplates that the mission takes place in the late spring. During this period, England and Europe experience extremely long hours of daylight. The itinerary explains what happens before the combat crews are involved; what is required of the combat crews in just getting ready to fly, and what is required after the mission is completed. The itinerary does not purport to represent any one particular mission, but in a measure it represents all of them.

The mission really starts the day before when Eighth Air Force headquarters studies weather patterns, prospective targets, crew availability, plane availability and a myriad of other factors. Decisions are made and notice is sent to each combat group. This notice can be "Stand Down," which means there will be no mission the next day, "Stand By," which means there will probably be a mission—be ready to act, or a "Loading," which means there will be a mission the next day.

This notice includes all the information concerning the mission; the type of bombs to be carried, the target, the amount of fuel to be carried, the number of ships the group is expected to launch, the time schedule, and many other details too numerous to record here. This loading is received by the group in the late afternoon or more likely in the evening. The combat crews are notified that there is a mission the next day and who is scheduled to fly. This motivates the crew man to retire early, usually right after dinner. The club and bar are not busy this night and there is an air of expectancy on the base. The crews which have been selected for the mission were picked by the operations office of each squadron.

The day of the mission runs generally as follows:

| | |
|---|---|
| 1:30 AM | **WAKE UP.** The crews are roused, told the time and what time breakfast will be served. They are also told what time Briefing will be, so the crews can plan their time. |
| 2 - 2:30 AM | **BREAKFAST.** The combat breakfast is a special one. It consists of juice, cereal, FRESH EGGS, pancakes, sausage, bacon, ham, home fries, grits, and coffee. Occasionally, a combat crew man not on the mission will get up and come to breakfast just to have the fresh eggs. |
| 2:30 - 3:30 AM | **BRIEFING.** This is a meeting of all combat crews scheduled to fly today's mission. It is conducted in an auditorium like building near the flight line. Security is very tight. Only those crews on the loading are admitted. As the crews enter, they deposit all personal items such as jewelry, pictures, letters, and just about anything beyond their dog tags (which display only the crewman's name, serial number, date of birth, blood type, and religion). The deposit of all personal items is done to avoid giving the enemy any information in the event the crewman is shot down and taken prisoner. When all combat crews are assembled, the doors are locked and no one is allowed to enter until the briefing is completed and all confidential material has been secured. |

After the room has been secured, the briefing begins. On the wall in the front of the room is displayed a large map of England and Europe. Until the room is secured, the map is covered by a shade. After all combat crews have been seated, the map is uncovered. On the map, a colored ribbon has been placed to outline the route to be followed to the target. Also on the map are areas shaded in red to indicate the presence of heavy flak batteries. Flak is the shrapnel from the exploding shells fired by the anti-aircraft guns. These have timed fuses to explode at the planes altitude. The course outlined by the ribbon is planned to avoid the flak barrages and fighter interception. The unveiling of the map is dramatic for the combat crews. They react very vocally. If the ribbon runs to a known difficult target, the reaction is one of groans; if it runs to a target which is expected to be easy, there are whistles and cheers. These quickly subside and the briefing continues.

Among the matters discussed is weather—where we can expect any fronts, how high the clouds will be, what the weather will be at the target, will the target be in the clear, or will there be partial covering. The weather man comments on whether or not contrails can be expected. Contrails are the condensation trails left by engine exhausts. These can be seen from the ground with the naked eye whereas the plane cannot be seen without binoculars. The contrails are bothersome to the pilots since they tend to induce vertigo from staring at them. Comments are also made regarding the possibility of icing during the climb through the clouds.

The crews are told what fighter escort they can expect, what type of fighters, how many, and how far they will accompany our group on the way in, and where they will meet us on our return. The briefer will try to forecast what fighter attacks we will meet, and where they will occur. This is based on whatever intelligence reports are available. It is seldom accurate, and is at best, a guess.

The bomb load is described, telling the crews what type of bombs will be carried, whether they will be incendiary or general purpose. Some ships may carry a load called "Nickels." Nickels are propaganda literature dropped along with the bombs for the Germans to read. The crews generally don't like to carry nickles. They think it is foolish to risk life to carry propaganda. Radio frequencies, call signs, and a myriad of other items are distributed. One of the very important things is the time check. Every flying officer has been issued a "hack watch." This is a special watch on which it is possible to stop every hand including the sweep second hand so that every watch has the exact same correct time. Escape kits are distributed. These are to help the crew man if shot down. These include some money of the type used in the countries over which the mission will fly. The kit also includes a head and shoulders picture of the crew man in civilian clothing. This would be used to make an identification card if the crew man was picked up by the Resistance or the Underground. There is a map, printed on silk, of the area over which the flight would take place and a compass which would be valuable if traveling over rural ground. The escape kit was returned after every mission. Large scale pictures were shown depicting the target with landmarks pointed out and cautions given where camouflage was known to exist. Any other information pertinent to the target or the flight path is given and the navigators, bombardiers, and radio operators are released to go to their respective briefings. The gunners go to the armament shack to pick up the guns. At the same time, the gunners obtain a truck, load on the guns, flak suits and extra ammunition. When the pilot, co-pilot, navigator, bombardier and radio operator are ready, they join the gunners, and all ride out to the plane together.

3:30 - 6:00 AM     **Get ready time.** During this period, the crew dons their combat clothing. This will vary from man to man, but basically it consists of long underwear, uniform, electrically heated suit, coveralls, wool socks, Mae West life preserver, and parachute harness. The gunners in the unprotected parts of the plane additionally wear fleece lined outer garments and whatever else they think they need. The gunners have also picked up the combat rations. For each crew man this consists of two cookies, one candy bar, and a pack of gum. The gum is very important because when breathing oxygen, it is necessary to breath through the mouth, and lots of saliva is necessary to moisten the throat. Chewing the gum promotes this.

At the plane, much needs to be done. The gunners must install their guns and check to make sure there is adequate ammunition. The bombardier must check the bomb load which had been loaded by the ground crew, the mechanisms pertinent to their storage during flight and their release over the target. The navigator gets his station ready to go. The pilot, assisted by the co-pilot and the engineer, check the entire plane and cover in detail every thing with the ground crew chief. When the pilot decides every thing is in order and ready for combat, the crew boards the plane and is ready for the "Start Engines" flare.

| | |
|---|---|
| 6:00 AM | Flare to start engines. |
| 6:10 AM | Flare to taxi to position for take off. |
| 6:20 AM | **Take off.** |
| 6:20 AM<br>4:30 PM | **Combat flight to target, bomb and return.** (This will be descried in Combat Mission) |
| 4:30 - 6:00 PM | **De-briefing.** The entire crew joins an interrogator to review the entire day's flight. Anything out of the ordinary is reported as well as everything about a fighter attack, such as make of fighters, identifying markings, method of attack, number of fighters, number of enemy fighters destroyed, location of attack, duration of attack, and intensity of attack. Those crew members who are in position to observe, report bombing results. Every detail, no matter how small or insignificant it may seem must be reported. Information regarding flak barrages is given with details as to the intensity and accuracy with emphasis on how accurately they had estimated our altitude. The intelligence officer will probe about anything different being reported by other crews to make sure nothing is forgotten or overlooked. |

6:00 - 7:00 PM **Dinner.** Either before or after dinner the gunners must go to the armament shack and clean their guns and make them ready for the next mission.

7:00 PM **Bed**

*James J. "Reddo" Redmond, Jr.*

# THE COMBAT MISSIONS

## MISSION NUMBER 01: CAEN, FRANCE
FEBRUARY 6, 1944
BOMBERS LOST: 6

This is it. We are really going into combat. We have trained for a year for this and now here it is. This will be our first mission and we don't know what to expect. All the crew is excited and a little scared. We have observed the experienced crews. They are casual but quiet. They have seen the elephant (this describes those who have been in combat and experienced its horrors). We all got up immediately on being called, but we did not seem to have enough time to complete everything and be ready for take off. We were just barely ready when the start engines flare was shot off. At briefing, we found that our target was Dijon, France. It was not surprising that our target was in France because the Eighth Air Force had been restricted from missions deep into Germany as the result of the terrible beatings it took in missions to Schweinfurt and Regensburg, in late autumn 1943.

Dijon is in the very south of France. Our trip to Dijon took about four hours. We were shot at a number of times as we passed cities that had flak batteries. It was hard to believe that this was the enemy and they were shooting at us. We had fighter escort for only the first few minutes of the mission. This escort was furnished by the RAF flying Spitfires which had only enough range to cross the channel and spend a few minutes over France. The rest of the way we had to go it alone. We did not get attacked by German fighters on the way to Dijon, but we had plenty of time to think about them and worry about them. All the crew members had to be alert and constantly scan the sky looking for enemy fighters. We had been warned about how short the time was from the time an enemy fighter was sighted until he was attacking. No matter how much training we had received, combat is an unknown until it has been experienced.

When we got to Dijon, we found the target covered by clouds, and in France we were not allowed to bomb unless we could clearly see and identify the target. We did not bomb and started back toward England, looking for an alternate target. We found a rail center near Caen, and with good visibility, bombed it. Caen was heavily protected by flak batteries and gave us a good barrage. We thought the barrage was heavy but the experienced crews said it was light. We were attacked by thirty or forty enemy fighters mostly ME-109s and FW-190s. Since we were close to the channel, we were now met by the RAF fighters and the Germans broke off and left. We were greatly relieved. This is real combat and we are in the major leagues. This is really exciting. We now consider ourselves to be combat experienced.

After briefing and dinner, we were talking about the mission and realized that we did not consider the damage we inflicted on our target or the people who were injured or killed by our bombing. Our only thought was to destroy the target and bring the war to a victorious close.

The mission took about eight hours and we were exhausted. We went to bed right after dinner, who knows what tomorrow will bring.

## MISSION NUMBER 02: LEIPZIG, GERMANY
FEBRUARY 20, 1944
BOMBERS LOST: 25

This was the first mission deep into Germany since the disastrous mission on "Black Thursday" in October 1943. The Eighth Air Force had been restricted from making any deep penetrations into Germany until fighter support could be provided for at least a portion of the trip. Although the combat crews were not aware, this would be the start of the major assault by the

Eighth Air Force against the Lufftwaffe.  With unprecedented good weather, the Eighth Air Force was able to fly five missions in the next six days.  This was later to become known as "Big Week."

This mission was nothing like our first mission.  We were attacked by dozens of enemy fighters, both ME-109s and FW-190s.  I don't know how many of our bombers were shot down, I was too busy to observe.  Probably a lot.

This was the first mission on which we would have fighter escort.  The P-47s and P-38s had arrived and would escort us on this mission.  However, their range was short and they could not escort us all the way to the target.  When their fuel was exhausted they would have to turn back to England and we would continue on alone to the target.  The Germans recognized what was happening and avoided attacking us until the escorting fighters had turned back.  Then they attacked in force.  We had a running battle with them for about an hour or an hour and a half until we reached the target and started on our bomb run.  The fighters broke off at that point as we entered the heavy flak barrage.

I suspected that the German fighters had landed, refueled, replenished ammunition, and were ready for us when we completed the bomb run.  As we completed the bomb run and left the heavy flak area, the German fighters were ready and waiting for us.  They attacked with renewed vigor and the battle continued until we met our escorting fighters.  When they showed up the Germans broke off and the battle was over.  This part of the fight lasted about an hour and we were subjected to attack from all directions, but most attacks came from dead ahead (twelve o'clock level).

On one of the attacks from head on, one of the ME-109s came through the formation, tipped up on a wing and as he passed me, the top of his canopy was toward me.  As he passed, he saluted.  I was startled; I had not expected any such thing.  My thoughts brought me back to the pulp magazines I read as a kid about air combat in world war one, when air combat was chivalrous, and pilots would salute one another as they shot each other down. It was over before I could return the salute. I wondered who he was, what kind of guy he was, and whether we might have been friends under other circumstances.

While I did not observe how many bombers were shot down, our plane was so situated in the formation that I could see Dick Nelson's plane. He was a pilot with whom I had gone through combat crew phase training. He was in the low squadron. Our plane was in the high squadron. I had a good view of the attack on Nelson's plane. I happened to be looking right at Nelson's plane when a twenty millimeter cannon shell exploded in the cockpit. Of course I could not see anything more than the flash of the explosion. I could not know what happened to the men in the cockpit. I later found out that the explosion killed Bartley, the co-pilot, and seriously wounded Dick Nelson the pilot. The last I saw of the plane was when they salvoed their bombs, left the formation and went into a spiral. Members of my crew reported seeing one chute come out of the plane. I later found out that it was the bombardier who bailed out. I believe he was taken prisoner. We went on to bomb the target.

Dick Nelson was the first of my close friends to be shot down within my sight, but war in the air is so impersonal that sensitivities are dulled and you go on fighting the war without a backward look. It was both Nelson's and my second mission flown.

On our return to our base at Polebrook, we learned that although the bombardier had bailed out over Germany and the plane was in a spiral, the top turret gunner had come out of his turret and was able to pull the plane out of the spiral to some semblance of level flight. The navigator, Lt. Walter Truemper and Sgt Archie Mathies, the ball turret operator came out of their positions and the two of them flew the crippled bomber back to England. We, with the rest of the group, got back about the same time as the crippled ship. All the bombers were instructed to not land at Polebrook, but to land at any other field. Truemper and Mathies were instructed to bail the crew out over Polebrook, then aim the ship out to sea, and bail out themselves. They did bail the crew out, but refused to jump themselves saying that Nelson was alive and they wanted to save him. Neither had any pilot training but they attempted two landings. On the first attempt, Col. Romig and Col. Le Doux tried to fly along side and guide them in, but the crippled plane very nearly crashed into them. On their last attempt, they tried to land in a field but due to their total lack of experience, crashed. Both Truemper and Mathies were killed instantly, but Nelson was still alive when removed from the wreckage. He died later that day. Lt. Walter Truemper and Sgt Archie Mathies were each awarded the Congressional Medal of Honor; I watched the whole thing and will never forget it.

The story of this tragedy has been preserved in a book entitled "Valor at Polebrook" written by Rick School and Jeff Rogers. It tells in detail the whole story to which I was privileged to be an eye witness.

It is impossible to describe the emotions that flow over you when something like this occurs. It is so different to see personal friends fighting for their lives and losing. This was personal, although in aerial combat with the enemy, life and death are quite impersonal.

The following page shows the bombing formation for this mission and was reproduced from the book "Valor at Polebrook."

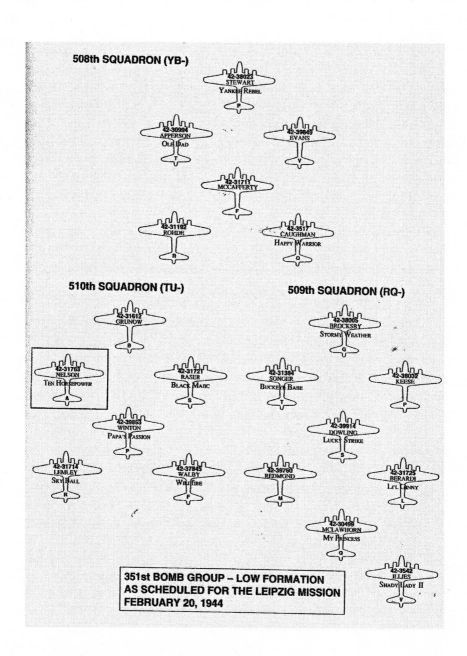

508th SQUADRON (YB-)

42-38023 STEWART
YANKEE REBEL
P

42-30994 APPERSON
OLE DAD
T

42-39849 EVANS
V

42-31711 McCAFFERTY
F

42-31192 ROHDE
R

42-3517 CAUGHMAN
HAPPY WARRIOR
Q

510th SQUADRON (TU-)

42-31612 GRUNOW
B

42-31763 NELSON
TEN HORSEPOWER
A

42-31721 RASER
BLACK MAGIC
S

42-39953 WINTON
PAPA'S PASSION
P

42-31714 LEMLEY
SKY BALL
R

42-37845 WALBY
WILDFIRE
F

42-39760 REDMOND
M

509th SQUADRON (RQ-)

42-38005 BROCKSBY
STORMY WEATHER
G

42-31364 SONGER
BUCKEYE BABE
T

42-38032 KEESE
P

42-39914 DOWLING
LUCKY STRIKE
S

42-31725 BERARDI
LI'L GINNY
L

42-30499 McLAWHORN
MY PRINCESS
Q

42-3542 ILLIES
SHADY LADY II
V

351st BOMB GROUP – LOW FORMATION
AS SCHEDULED FOR THE LEIPZIG MISSION
FEBRUARY 20, 1944

## MISSION NUMBER 03: ACHMER, GERMANY
FEBRUARY 21, 1944
BOMBERS LOST: 23

We were briefed for Gutersloh, Germany, but the cloud cover was 10/10 (complete). It was necessary to find another target. We found the Lufftwaffe Base at Achmer was in the clear, so we prepared to bomb it. As we entered on the bombing run, it was like disturbing a hornet's nest because their fighters came up in droves to attack us. This was terrifying. This is two days in a row that our planes are being knocked out of the sky as though they were targets in a shooting gallery. Flying twenty-five missions looks a lot harder now than it did on our first mission. Flak was very heavy and accurate over the target. Our Group lost five or six planes out of the sixteen that made the mission. I would guess that our losses were evenly divided between fighters' attacks and flak.

There were additional losses that occurred on take off before the mission got off the ground. Two planes were unable to get airborne. One of these was piloted by my best friend all through training, Bud Ritzema. He had a runaway prop and was unable to get airborne. Fortunately he did not crash, he just ran off the end of the runway. There was no fire or explosion and there were no injuries among his crew. The other plane was apparently not developing full power and although it did get airborne it could not gain altitude. It was flying about treetop level when it crashed. The plane exploded and all ten crew men were killed.

I knew that Ritzema was not with the formation but I had no idea what had happened to him. I was happy to have dinner with him that night and hear from him what had happened on take off. We knew that he was on the loading for a mission the next morning, but never suspected that this would be his first and last mission, or that we would never see each other again. Ritzema's mission the next day was to Magdeburg. He did not get to the target, but was shot down by flak over the Ruhr Valley. He was missed at dinner that night and for some time to come. As time passed, I often wondered what had happened to Ritz. I never knew whether he had been killed or taken prisoner.

## MISSION NUMBER 04: SCHWEINFURT, GERMANY
FEBRUARY 24, 1944
BOMBERS LOST: 46

We were all scared about this one: it was the most infamous target in Europe. This would be the first time the Eighth Air Force would return to Schweinfurt since the devastating raid in October, now known as "Black Thursday." In that raid twenty percent of the bombers were shot down and there was serious concern as to the feasibility of continuing the bombing program. After that mission, the bombing program was restricted from making long missions into Germany. This restriction continued until February 1944, when the P-47 and the P-38 fighter planes came into service. Although they did not have the range to accompany the bombers to the target, they could offer protection part way and the bombing program was resumed as before.

At briefing, when the shade was lifted from the map and the target could be seen, I think every heart skipped a beat. However, "Ours not to reason why, ours but to do or die," we got ready to go. Perhaps because we expected the mission to be so terrible, it didn't seem so bad. We were attacked by fifty or sixty fighters, ME-109s and FW190s. Flak was medium to heavy and was very accurate. We lost two planes out of sixteen but severe damage was sustained by many of the others. I guess we were lucky because while we only lost two planes, I could see other groups that were taking a beating.

Wow! Three missions in four days. I was pooped and still tired when I got up in the morning. I have lost ten pounds in the last four days. My crew has not complained but I know these men, and I know from the expression on their faces that they are exhausted and need rest.

## MISSION NUMBER 05: WILHELMSHAVEN, GERMANY
MARCH 3, 1944
BOMBERS LOST: 14

We were briefed for Erkner, Germany. The weather was forecast to be bad, but it was much worse than expected. I sometimes wonder if the weather men know what they are doing. Cloud cover over the target was 10/10, and a front extended so high, that we could never have gotten over it with a bomb load. We were being led by a pathfinder plane which had bombing equipment that enabled them to bomb through clouds. Wilhelmshaven was selected as an alternate target and we bombed it. There were no enemy fighters. (I guess they could not get off the ground because of the weather). Flak was light and not very accurate. As usual, we had fighter support for only part of the mission.

We keep hearing about the new P-51s that are supposed to be arriving, but we have yet to see one. This business of not having escort for the farthest part of the mission is getting a little old. I suppose they will get here eventually. I hope we have all survived and are here to welcome them.

## MISSION NUMBER 06: BERLIN, GERMANY
MARCH 4, 1944
BOMBERS LOST: 16

When we entered the briefing room no one, as usual, had any idea what the target was. We noted that the room was crowded with camera men and reporters. We knew that something was up and we wondered among ourselves what it might be. When the shade was rolled up and the target was revealed, the room was a mad house. Our first reaction was that no one would survive such a mission but after a moment or two we realized that we were being given the honor of leading the first daylight raid on Berlin.

We were very proud and more than a little scared of leading the first American daylight bombing mission to Berlin.

After a few minutes, the room settled down to the serious business of the briefing. The pop of flash bulbs continued throughout the briefing. As we went about the business of getting ready to go, there was a high level of excitement which dissipated as the time for take off approached. When we were in the air it was just like any other mission.

The weather forecast had not been good and the actual weather was much worse than forecast. We ran into a weather front about an hour short of the target and we had to circle to try to get enough altitude to get over the front. We were gaining altitude so slowly that it became apparent that we could not top this front with our bomb load. We approached 30,000 feet before we abandoned Berlin as a target. We could see the B-24s milling about, 3,000 or 4,000 feet lower than us. They were having trouble maintaining formation.

The decision was made to select an alternate target and we selected Bonn but it was a disappointment for the crews not to be the first to bomb Berlin. The next day or so some other group will be selected to be the first. We had missed our opportunity.

Other than the weather, and missing our opportunity to be the first to bomb Berlin, the mission was quite ordinary. There were no enemy fighters. I guess the weather was so bad that they couldn't take off. Again, the flak was light and inaccurate. When we returned to Polebrook and de-briefing, the reporters and camera men were all gone. There was no jubilation. There was no excitement It was a routine debriefing attended by the disappointed crewmen.

## MISSION NUMBER 07: ERKNER, GERMANY
MARCH 8, 1944
BOMBERS LOST: 40

This target is a suburb of Berlin. Our route took us near Hanover and in this area we were attacked by forty to fifty enemy fighters. These were mostly ME-109s with a few FW-190s and JU-87s. Several FW-189s attempted air to air bombing. Some attacks were made from above and head on but most were made from below because we had good fighter support.

As we approached the Erkner-Berlin area, there were no fighter attacks on us and Brigadier General Travis came on the radio to issue a challenge to the Lufftwaffe. His message was "This is Brigadier General Travis with the Eighth Air Force over the heart of Berlin. Why don't you come up and fight? Why don't you protect the Fatherland?" I nearly popped my lid. No way did I want the Lufftwaffe to come up and fight. Maybe we were lucky or maybe we had been observed flying good formation but in any event, we were not attacked. The Lufftwaffe concentrated on other groups. I later found out that the Eighth Air Force had suffered heavy losses.

Flak was unbelievable. It was the heaviest I had ever seen and it was extremely accurate. Most planes took serious damage, but none of the 351st bomb group planes were lost over the continent.

The only man in the crew who would be aware of General Travis' radio transmission was the pilot. The gunners would be on the intercom. The co-pilot would be alternating between the intercom and traffic between planes in our group formation. The pilot would monitor traffic from the command ship, and listen in from time to time on other channels.

After the mission there was much bitching among the pilots about General Travis' transmission. As usual, all we could do was bitch among ourselves. Later on we found out that the over all strategy was to tempt the German fighters up to fight because it was anticipated that we would soon have an overwhelming superiority in fighters over them and it was the strategic aim to destroy the Lufftwaffe before the invasion of France. Like it or not, we were being used as bait to attract the Lufftwaffe up to fight.

## MISSION NUMBER 08: BERLIN, GERMANY
MARCH 9, 1944
BOMBERS LOST: 69

This weather is something else. We came all this distance only to find Berlin covered by clouds. Bombing was done by Pathfinder. We have no idea as to whether any damage was done, or if we even hit the target. The recco (reconnaissance) planes will have to get pictures when the weather clears up.

We were expecting a rough mission but we did not see even one German fighter. I know they were active because I could hear the combat conversation on the radio. I found out later that there were heavy losses sustained by the Eighth Air Force. The only explanation can be that we were flying good formation and the enemy passed us up for more attractive targets. The flak was intense and super accurate but some how the 351st escaped serious damage. Most planes took hits but none were critical. Losses were heavy for other groups.

## MISSION NUMBER 09: MUNSTER, GERMANY
MARCH 11, 1944
BOMBERS LOST: 29

I don't know why we were not very impressed with this target at briefing. It could be a very difficult mission or it could be a "Milk Run." Milk Run was the name given by the combat crews to a mission which turns out to be very easy. Maybe our cavalier attitude was the result of having flown a lot of missions in a short period of time.

*James J. "Reddo" Redmond, Jr.*

This mission turned out to be a milk run. The target was covered by clouds and bombing was done by Pathfinder. We could not observe what results we achieved.

Flak over the target was very heavy but not very accurate. A number of planes were hit, but none of our planes were lost. We did not see any Lufftwaffe fighter planes but radio chatter indicated that some groups were having a bad time.

## MISSION NUMBER 10: FRANKFURT, GERMANY
MARCH 20, 1944
BOMBERS LOST: 8

At briefing, the weather people said that weather might be bad over the continent. They were right. Over France we ran into a front that soared up to over 28,000 feet. It would be very difficult to get over and we could not get a sighting on any target. Over France, we were not allowed to bomb unless we could find a military target and positively identify it. The mission was recalled and we brought our load of bombs back to Polebrook.

This was the first time I had to land with a full load of bombs. I sent Tony Wagner back to the bomb bay to be sure the bombs were secure in their racks and safe. It was very ticklish but that B-17 just settled in like it was something done every day.

There was very accurate medium flak over the enemy coast both on the way in and on the way home. These flak gunners on the enemy coast are very good because they get to practice on us on every mission. Most planes took some damage but we lost none. We saw no fighters.

## MISSION NUMBER 11: BERLIN, GERMANY
MARCH 22, 1944
BOMBERS LOST: 13

We were briefed for Oriensburg as a visual target, but as so frequently happens, it was under heavy cloud cover. From radio transmissions we found out that Berlin was clear, so we went to Berlin. We bombed with good results. We were not attacked by enemy fighters, although we did see several groups of them. They just looked our formation over and passed us up. Apparently they were looking for a group flying poor formation, and went on to attack some other group. Some groups reported heavy fighter attacks. Flak was extremely heavy and accurate.

We lost one plane but many were heavily damaged. I have no idea about what happened to those who reported heavy fighter attacks.

While the mission was fairly mild, we had something happen that is always worrisome to the crew. We had a 500 pound bomb that did not release from the plane when the bombardier dropped it. After "Bombs Away" the radio operator is required to look into the bomb bay to make sure that all bombs have left the plane. On this occasion, Lloyd Bogle, the radio operator reported that there was one bomb still in the bomb bay partially released and hanging from one connector. Since the bombardier is responsible, Tony Wagner put on his parachute, clipped on a walk around oxygen bottle, took his tools and went into the open bomb bay to try to release the bomb. He reported that the arming device had been activated and the bomb was live. That meant that if the bomb was jolted from its position and struck some part of the plane it could explode. It was a very difficult job to release the bomb. Tony had to work in the open bomb bay, hang over the open doors, hampered by his bulky parachute, and oxygen bottle to make the release. One slip and Tony would make a 24,000 foot parachute jump into Germany.

The bomb had to be released because we could not possibly land with a live bomb hanging in the bomb bay. Tony was an excellent bombardier and knew his business. It took only a short time, maybe fifteen minutes, to release the bomb but it seemed like forever to the rest of the crew. Everyone was elated when Tony announced "Bombs Away" and closed the bomb bay doors.

To appreciate how difficult a job this is, remember that we are at 24,000 feet. The temperature this day was 40 degrees below zero. It was necessary for him to have a walk around oxygen bottle, wear his parachute and brace himself against the girders in the bomb bay to keep from falling out, all the while trying to release the bomb. Tony was the hero of the day, and we all told him so when we got back.

## MISSION NUMBER 12: MUNSTER, GERMANY
MARCH 23, 1944
BOMBERS LOST: 29

We were briefed for Lippstadt, Germany, but the target was covered by clouds. We altered our course to Munster, Germany. This was our alternate target. The flak at this target was super heavy and very accurate. It was so accurate that our number four engine (right outboard) was hit and set on fire. Fire in the air is terrifying. We had over two thousand gallons of high octane gas in our wing tanks only inches from the fire in the engine. An explosion was imminent. We had to get out of the formation at once because if we blew up, we might take other planes with us. We had only one chance and that was to dive the plane and hope the fire gets blown out.

Free of the formation, with the number 4 prop feathered, I dived steep and fast. The crew could not know what to expect. They knew we had a fire and they were terrified. There was no time to tell them what to expect. In the dive, they were thrown up against the roof of the plane. Fortunately all were wearing steel helmets which protected their heads. One crew man later said he was plastered up against the roof for minutes. Luckily none of the crew was hurt. I guess God was with us because the dive extinguished the fire. The engine was still smoking but there were no flames. I was still concerned about this fearing that it might burst into flames again. Fortunately, it did not.

We had just recovered from this fire when our number 1 engine (left outboard) was hit by flak. It did not catch fire, but it was out of service. We had now lost both outboard engines and flying with the two inboard engines we were not able to maintain altitude even after dropping our bombs. We probably plowed some German farmer's potato patch or maybe flattened his out house.

Now we had a new problem. We were not flying our regular plane because it was having battle damage repaired and the plane we were flying did not have Tokyo tanks. Tokyo tanks are fuel tanks built into the wing tips which add about 1,000 gallons to the fuel capacity. We were carrying about 500 gallons of fuel less than the other planes in the formation. The gas we were carrying would have been plenty if we had all four engines.

This became two problems. First: Do we have enough fuel to make it back to England? And second, if we do have enough fuel, do we have enough altitude? We were losing altitude steadily. I asked Marty Strom our navigator where was the closest place to head for. I was hoping he would say lets go to Sweden where he had relatives and we would be interned and watch the rest of the war. Marty said the only place available to us was England. Our present position was south and east of the Ruhr Valley which was a major industrial area for the Germans. The flak barrages the Ruhr Valley could put up were terrifying. Marty did a magnificent job of threading our way through and around the flak. We had just gotten through the heavy flak area when several ME-109s appeared. They were approaching and getting into position for an attack. They look for cripples such as we because we would be easy pickings. I thought it was all over but the shouting, when I was able to contact an American fighter pilot. He said he would be right there. I had no idea where he was. None of the crew had seen him either, but almost immediately three P-38s appeared out of nowhere and the ME-109s scrammed. The P-38s escorted us until their fuel ran low, when they were relieved by three P-47s, who stayed with us until we reached the enemy coast.

Now all we had to worry about was fuel and altitude. Cavanaugh was nursing a cold so we had a substitute co-pilot. He was a Nervous Nellie. He was upsetting the crew with his continuous reports over the intercom that we did not have enough gas or altitude to reach England. I finally told him to sit quiet, shut up and stop upsetting the crew. You could almost see the fuel gauges moving toward empty because of the high power settings I was using. I was pulling 56 inches of manifold pressure on both inboard engines, and we were barely maintaining flying speed (maximum manifold pressure allowed is 46 inches on take off for a time limit of five minutes). I was afraid that at any time one or both engines would quit or explode. They didn't, but both engines were ruined. All four engines had to be replaced.

At long last we got back, not only to England, but to our base at Polebrook. Our landing would have to be perfect on the first attempt. We did not have enough power to go around and make a second attempt. We came in and touched down on the first third of the runway, and rolled to a stop.

The whole group had gone on to the target, bombed and returned to base. They were back a full hour before we made an appearance. Debriefing was over when we walked into the briefing room. Every one was surprised. We had been reported as missing in action, and there were two eye witness reports that they saw us explode and blow up as we left the formation. We were all glad this one was over. We went to dinner and found out there was a mission scheduled for the next day and we were on the loading. We went to bed right after dinner, tomorrow might be rough.

## MISSION NUMBER 13: SCHWEINFURT, GERMANY
MARCH 24, 1944
BOMBERS LOST: 8

This is the second time we are scheduled to go to Schweinfurt. It really scares the hell out of us. All we can think of is the beating the Eighth Air Force took at this target only a few months ago. They suffered losses of 20%. Five such missions would eliminate the Eighth Air Force from combat. As we got ready to go, the crew was very quiet, much more so than on any other mission. I guess they are afraid it will be a very rough mission.

We were surprised and a little happy that the cloud cover was even worse than had been forecast. The clouds reached all the way to the ground and prevented the enemy fighters from coming up to attack us. They would be able to take off but not able to land. Thank you God for favors. We did not see one enemy fighter during the whole mission. We were attacked by flak at several places along the route both on the way in and on the way out. The flak we experienced was not very heavy or accurate.

We bombed through total cloud cover so results could not be observed. Wow! Again four missions in five days! Once again, I am pooped. I gained back the weight I lost before and now again I have lost another ten pounds. I am concerned for my crew but this is a blue ribbon crew. They threw fatigue aside and continued to function like champions. There is no mission scheduled for tomorrow so we can rest and recuperate and be ready for whatever is in store for us.

## MISSION NUMBER 14: WATTEN, FRANCE
MARCH 26, 1944
BOMBERS LOST: 6

This target was on the French Coast, so we knew it would be a short mission. We consider these missions on the coast as easy ones because we seldom encounter enemy fighters. This is

119

because we usually have good fighter escort. Even the RAF Spitfires can escort us there, and they were our escort today. No enemy fighters appeared.

The flak gunners on the coast are very good because they get lots of practice. No matter where the target is your route takes you over the coastal guns. They cannot be avoided. They get a shot at you both on the way in and again on the way back to England. On this trip, flak knocked out our number one engine (left outboard) but since we had no fire and were so close to the channel and home, we had no real concern. We feathered the prop, left the formation, and had a nice slow ride back to Polebrook. The flak was quite heavy and accurate. About half of the planes in our group suffered damage in varying amounts.

## MISSION NUMBER 15: TOURS, FRANCE
MARCH 27, 1944
BOMBERS LOST: 11

This was a milk run. We just love these short trips into France. Time wise they are of short duration, there is not a lot of hazard and we rarely see any German Fighters and very important they count toward completion of your tour. We did not encounter even one German fighter. It was a beautiful day, clear of almost all clouds. Our bombing was excellent. We could see the results on the air field that was our target. Several large hangers were destroyed and a number of buildings were set on fire. There were craters on the main runway as well as the main highway into Tours.

As usual, we encountered flak near Le Havre, it was neither heavy or accurate. The crew commented on this and suggested that the flak gunners must have been in town. They all volunteered to contribute some money to keep them there.

## MISSION NUMBER 16: BRUNSWICK, GERMANY
MARCH 29, 1944
BOMBERS LOST: 10

Brunswick is usually a hot bed of flak and this mission was no exception. However, the flak gunners were hampered by total cloud cover and had to aim by radar. They were not as accurate as usual. On our approach to the target we were attacked by twenty to thirty fighters, both ME-109 and FW-190s. But now something new occurred. The enemy fighters were lining up as though they were going to make a broadside attack on the formation, but instead of making a fighter attack, they stayed out of range of our 50 caliber machine guns, and started to fire rockets at us. This was the first time we ever saw this kind of attack and I do not believe that such an attack had ever been reported by any other group. The rockets were not very accurate since they did not hit any bombers or explode close enough to do extensive damage. Something like this is very scary when you have never seen it before. Bombing was done through a total under cast and bombing results could not be observed, although a large quantity of black smoke was seen coming up through the clouds.

England is noted for its bad weather, but the weather we experienced on our return was unbelievable. The whole of south east England was blanketed with a cloud cover extending from about 200 feet up to 9,000 feet. It was impossible to fly formation because the clouds were too thick. At an altitude of 200 feet it was possible to see the ground but there was no horizontal vision. There were about 1,000 bombers milling about in this soup with no one able to see anyone else. At one time, a B-17 passed over us and missed us by about 15 feet. Ordinarily it is not possible to hear another plane in flight but this time the roar of the engines was deafening. I looked up as he passed over us and we were so close that I could see the rivets on the bottom of his plane. He never saw us and never knew we were there. He never knew that he almost died that day.

We located the field and were making a straight in approach. We had not yet seen the runway but were positioning ourselves by a marker located mile or two short of the runway. We had the wheels down and flaps half way down, when another B-17 dropped out of the soup right in front of us and went in to land. We struggled through the prop wash, did a tight 360 and landed. Neither of these two planes saw us and never knew how close they came to crashing. This was probably as close as any one could come to buying the farm and not closing the deal. The scariest thing about this was that there was nothing you could do. It all depended on the other guy and he didn't even know you were there. We were all pretty shaken up when we landed. This was scary.

While we were critical of the planes that came so close to crashing into us, we have no idea that we may have nearly hit another plane—never knowing a plane was there and never knowing how close we came to dying that day. As difficult as it was for all the ships to find the base and land all the while not being able to see the other planes, through some miracle, all planes landed in record brief time.

## MISSION NUMBER 17: ARNSWALDE, GERMANY
APRIL 11, 1944
BOMBERS LOST: 69

This was a tremendously long mission. The target was actually on the Polish border. Our actual logged flight time was over 12 hours. The time in the air was so long that the supply of oxygen and fuel were critical. In order to make the oxygen last for the entire mission, it was necessary to fly a substantial portion of the mission at an altitude of 14,000 feet. At briefing, it was explained that the flak guns at Hanover and Brunswick (our route took us between these two cities) would not be able to cross their fire at this altitude. This caused great consternation among the combat crews, because we knew from experience that both Brunswick and Hanover were noted for their heavy accurate flak barrages. Fuel was so critical that after we had started and warmed up our engines, they were shut off and the gas trucks came by and topped off the tanks.

We flew the route as briefed and when we went between Brunswick and Hanover we found the flak to be super heavy and accurate. Once we had passed these two cities, we were attacked by swarms of fighters. The usual ME109 and FW 190s. Many bombers were shot down, and almost every plane had substantial damage. We were supposed to have good fighter support, but I guess they were busy elsewhere. We later heard that the Eighth Air Force lost 64 bombers.

If anything bad is going to happen, it will happen on the bomb run. When on the bomb run nothing can detract from attention to the run. As we passed the I P (Initial Point) and entered the bomb run, a flak shell exploded very close to the plane. The noise was deafening and the whole plane shuddered. Simultaneous with this, Frank Cavanaugh, my co-pilot lunged foreword toward the wheel. I saw him out of the corner of my eye, and thought he was going to fall on the wheel. I braced preparing for the jolt but he did not touch the wheel. He remained hunched over. The cockpit was filled with pieces of kapok, as the vacuum created by the flak sucked out the entire contents of his seat back cushion. It was like one of those desk top novelties which when inverted make a snow storm inside the bowl. I jokingly commented after the mission that there were so many feathers flying around the cockpit that I couldn't see the instruments.

The bomb run required my undivided attention and I flew it wondering if Cavanaugh were dead or wounded. He had not moved or spoken since he first lunged forward. I had no idea as to his condition. I could not check on him until the bombs were dropped and I could loosen up the formation. Then Cavanaugh came on the intercom to report that he thought he was wounded since he could feel the blood running down the crack of his ass (it was sweat). I had Wes Creech, the top turret gunner come out of his turret and check on Cavanaugh. After an inspection, he reported that Cavanaugh was not injured: that his parachute harness had been cut in half and his coveralls, his shirt, his pants, and his electrically heated suit all had a foot long rip.  His long underwear had a long runner snagged in it but Cavanaugh's skin had not been broken.  He did have a very large nasty looking bruise that covered his whole side.  The steel seat back had a hole torn in it that a bowling ball would pass through.  The flak ricocheted off the armor plate behind the seat and tore a huge hole in the side of the plane where it exited.  Cavanaugh was so shook up that he did not even notice that he had no heat coming from his electrically heated suit as we returned to Polebrook.  He was just glad to be alive.

To my knowledge the combat crews were never again asked to fly a mission so long that we could not fly at our usual altitude.


## MISSION NUMBER 18: KASSEL, GERMANY
APRIL 19, 1944
BOMBERS LOST: 6

We were attacked by flak barrages at various points on the way to the target, but this was mostly light and not very accurate.  On the bomb run and over the target the flak was very heavy and very accurate.  A spent piece of flak came through the plane and hit me on the second finger of my left hand.  It struck at the second knuckle.  On a bomb run, your attention cannot deviate from the formation and flying.  I sweated this out, not being able to investigate until the bombs were dropped.  I knew I was hit, but it really didn't hurt, so I guess I was casual about it.  After the bombs were dropped, I turned the plane over to Cavanaugh and investigated my "wound."  The piece of flak was sticking out of my finger through my glove.  I simply pulled it out and put it in one of my pockets, took my glove off, wrapped my finger with my handkerchief and put my glove back on.  It only bled a drop or two and did not cause me much discomfort.

There were a considerable number of wounded in some of the other planes and they kept our little hospital busy. Because of this, and the fact that my finger did not hurt, I did not go to the hospital. As a matter of fact, I had seen wounded crew men and I was a little embarrassed to show my finger so I said nothing. The next day we had a very short mission and after our return, I thought maybe I had better have my finger looked at. I went to the hospital and showed them my "wound." The medics thought I was kidding them. They called all the medics and doctors in the hospital and held a conference to determine how best to treat my "wound." They solemnly prescribed a band aid, take two aspirins, and don't call them in the morning. I was quite embarrassed and did not have the temerity to even make reference to this matter for a number of years.

On this mission many planes were damaged by flak. We sustained the usual hits, but nothing serious. No planes were lost. At one point we were inspected by a group of enemy fighters but since we were flying good formation they decided to look for an easier target. This has happened to us on previous occasions and it makes an indelible impression of the importance of flying good formation.

## MISSION NUMBER 19: LA GLACERIE, FRANCE
APRIL 20, 1944
BOMBERS LOST: 15

This target is in the Pas de Calais area. At this point, the coast of England is only about 20 miles from the coast of France. Our targets for this mission were the ramps which the Germans would use to launch the V-1 missiles. They were hard to hit because they were skeletal in design and were not easily detected. There were no enemy fighters sighted. The Lufftwaffe does not attempt to fight so close to the coast because our escort is too overwhelming. The bombing by our group was poor and when the pictures were developed, we got hell.

As usual the flak on the coast was extremely accurate and unbelievably heavy. Every plane in the formation took heavy damage but there were no planes lost. There were wounded combat crew members as usual.


## MISSION NUMBER 20: HAMM, GERMANY
APRIL 22, 1944
BOMBERS LOST: 30

As a combat mission, this one was quite ordinary. We did not see any enemy fighters. Flak was light and not very accurate. We could hardly believe that a mission into Germany could be so uneventful. However, it was not without tragedy at our base. One plane crashed on take off when the number 2 engine failed just as the plane lifted off the runway. The co-pilot accidentally feathered the prop on number one engine and with the plane barely off the ground it went into a steep left bank and stalled. The left wing tip struck the ground and the plane crashed. It immediately burst into flames and the entire crew was killed. It happened so fast that they never had a chance.

This mission was horrendous for a B-24 Group. For some reason, unknown to us, the mission was scheduled so late in the day that it would require a return to England after dark. We were all concerned with having to fly formation after dark. We were assured that it would be only a short time and with our running lights it would not be a problem. As the formations were returning across the channel to England, it was pitch dark and regardless of what they had said at the briefing formation flying was difficult.

The Germans, being very enterprising fellows, had observed us over Germany and knew the distance we had to go and the time it would take to reach England. They knew that it would be well after dark before we even crossed the channel. They also knew that in the dark it would be almost impossible to identify enemy planes since all would be using running lights. They also knew that the

American combat crews would not be expecting enemy planes and would not be alert to their presence.

The Germans scrambled a squadron of fighter-bombers, and as darkness became total, they joined formation with a group of B-24s and flew in formation with them across the channel right to the B-24 Base. The combat crew men on the B-24s were not alert for this kind of attack and even if they detected any strange planes in the formation, they would have had little reason to suspect that they were enemy. After all, they were almost home.

A further contributing factor to the debacle which was about to happen, was the custom of the combat crews to unload their guns and remove them from their mounts to save time after landing. The B-24 combat crews could not even defend themselves. They had no guns available.

As the B-24s approached their field and entered the traffic pattern, the Germans turned off their running lights and began shooting the B-24s down. A number of B-24s were shot down on their final approach. Allied Ground Control knew there were enemy planes in the sky over England, but they could not tell how many or where they were. Anti-aircraft batteries which were located near the Base were attempting to shoot down the Germans, but in the dark it was difficult for them to identify friend or foe. The B-24 pilots were instructed to open their bomb bay doors and turn on the bomb bay lights so the anti aircraft batteries could identify which was which. This was only partially successful because it also helped the Germans to find the B-24s.

There was absolute chaos with more than a dozen B-24s being shot down or crashing.

To my knowledge, the Eighth Air Force never again scheduled a mission where return would be planned after dark. I don't know about other crews, but my crew never again removed a gun from its mount until the plane was safely on the ground.

James J. "Reddo" Redmond, Jr.

## MISSION NUMBER 21: ERDING, GERMANY
APRIL 24, 1944
BOMBERS LOST: 55

This target is near Munich. This was a real long trip. Our actual flight time was well over ten hours. We were subjected to the usual flak barrages on the way in to the target, but this time they were not as heavy or accurate as they usually are. Minor damage was sustained by only a few planes. As we approached the target, we were intercepted by forty or fifty enemy fighters. They did not make a concentrated attack, but rather made isolated slashes at the formation. They did not seem to have their heart in it. None of our planes suffered serious damage from these attacks. However, on our return flight, as we passed over the French coast, we underwent a heavy accurate barrage from the coast batteries. Nine out of our sixteen planes were damaged severely. One plane was hit so badly that they could not make the few miles across the channel. They were forced to ditch in the channel. Fortunately they made it close to the English coast and Air Sea Rescue picked up all ten crew men.

Over the target, flak was fairly accurate and heavy, particularly on the bomb run. Everything seems to happen on the bomb run when you cannot take your attention from the formation. On this bomb run, about two minutes to "Bombs Away," something smashed into the bottom of my left foot so hard that my foot was knocked completely off the rudder pedal. I didn't know what had happened. The only thing I could compare this to was someone smashing a baseball bat into the sole of your foot. I got my foot back on the rudder pedal and continued to fly the airplane. I could not check on anything until the bombs had been dropped. During this period, even though it was only a couple of minutes it seemed an eternity. The thoughts pass through your mind like an avalanche. I experienced the thoughts of being wounded. I did not feel any pain. I thought this was a combination of my feet being so cold that there was no feeling in them and shock which I had heard about. All of this was OK with me since I couldn't do anything about it anyway, but I wondered how long it would be before pain started. Finally, the bombs were dropped. I loosened the formation and gave the plane to Cavanaugh and proceeded to examine my foot. I pulled off my flying boot and looked at the bottom of it. There was a piece of the heavy rubber bottom of the boot that had been scooped out as though a large table spoon had dug it out. It was apparent that a piece of flak had struck my foot a glancing blow and had ricocheted off into some other part of the plane. By the time it had struck me, it had already torn its way through the bottom of the plane, the floor of the navigator's compartment and the floor of the cockpit. Marty Strom, our navigator, heard the crash as the flak tore through his floor. He could hardly believe how close it had come to tearing him up.

I had been so concerned about being in pain during our five and a half hour flight back to England, that when I knew I was not injured, I didn't mind the cold. My nearly frozen feet almost felt good.

## MISSION NUMBER 22: BERLIN, GERMANY
MAY 7, 1944
BOMBERS LOST: 13

Some groups reported very heavy fighter attacks, but we did not experience any. Flak was intense and very accurate. Every ship took many hits but most were not of a serious nature. That is, except for one ship that was shot down. I knew that the ship was piloted by a Lt. Presley. He was on his first mission. I had never met him or to my knowledge ever seen him. He had just become a member of the 351st. As I saw his plane go down, I wondered who he was. There were chutes seen coming out of his plane. I had hoped he made it.

*James J. "Reddo" Redmond, Jr.*

## MISSION NUMBER 23: LUXENBURG, GERMANY
MAY 9, 1944
BOMBERS LOST: 10

This was an easy mission. There was a light fighter attack, but these German pilots did not seem to be serious. They did not press home their attack with the same vigor and tenacity that we have been accustomed to in the past. They would break off their attack before they were in close range. Is it possible that the German pilots we are encountering now are less experienced and are not too eager for combat?

The flak we encountered was light and not very accurate. Our bombing was not good. I think we actually missed the target. Our target was the marshalling yards. If our bombing was as bad as I think it was, they will probably send us back.

## MISSION NUMBER 24: LUXEMBURG, GERMANY
MAY 11, 1944
BOMBERS LOST: 10

Again to Luxemburg. As we suspected, our bombing the other day was terrible, so we were sent back. I think our bombing today was much better. I hope the pictures show a better result. It worries us when we are sent back to a target. We are always fearful that the Germans may be waiting for us.

This mission we encountered no fighters. The flak near the target was light and not very accurate. The coastal flak batteries put up their usual heavy, accurate barrage.

## MISSION NUMBER 25: MERSEBURG, GERMANY
MAY 12, 1944
BOMBERS LOST: 55

We had relatively light fighter attacks. The enemy fighters did not seem to be interested in forcing an attack home. This was

130

lucky for us because we were flying lousy formation. The reason that good formation is so important is that with good formation, hundreds of 50 caliber machine guns can be brought to bear on any attacking fighter. If the formation is not maintained properly, there are many areas where an attacking fighter can attack with impunity.

Ted Myers, flying in the second element of the lead squadron, could not or would not stay in position. He would just get into position when he would soar up and force me and my squadron out of position. If there had been any good Lufftwaffe pilots in the area, we could have been wiped out.

I reported at debriefing that I would not fly in any position where Myers was positioned forward of me. I guess that operations took notice of my complaint, because Myers was never again positioned where he could be a problem.

During the month of May, the missions seemed to be much easier. There were few fighter attacks. Those that did take place, did not seem to have the same vigor that they used to have. There are all kinds of speculations about when the invasion will take place. We, the members of my crew, are not interested in this speculation. We are interested only in completing our tour.

With the exception of the coastal batteries, flak was moderate but not very accurate. We suffered no losses and most planes suffered little damage. However, the radio traffic would seem to indicate that some groups were catching hell.

When we got back, after we had completed our review with the ground crew, we realized that we had just completed our twenty fifth mission. This should be the Holy Grail. We should be finished with combat. It did no good to consider what might have been. We are scheduled to fly five more missions, and if we are lucky we will survive them. It bothers us that several other crews have been shot down after completing twenty-five and before completing thirty. Our crew has accepted the extra missions philosophically, and expects to complete thirty. After a little bitching, the crew gathered up their things and went in to de-briefing.

## MISSION NUMBER 26: KIEL, GERMANY
MAY 22, 1944
BOMBERS LOST: 7

This was a sadly mixed up mission. It was forecast that the target would probably be covered to some extent by clouds, so we were being led by a pathfinder ship which could bomb through cloud cover. When we reached the target, it was covered by clouds, but as we approached it on the bomb run, the cloud cover dispersed and the target was plainly visible. The pathfinder plane was making the bomb run and bombed by their instruments. The bombs fell in an open field, nowhere near the target. As we watched the bombs explode in pasture land, we could clearly see the target. There was no fighter activity and the flak was very light. Maybe the Germans decided not to waste their ammunition on such incompetents.

## MISSION NUMBER 27: BERLIN, GERMANY
MAY 24, 1944
BOMBERS LOST: 34

Berlin seems to be a favorite target for the Eighth Air Force. If my memory is correct, this is our fourth mission to this city. It must be a mess. We saw some enemy fighters who flew by and looked us over but decided to look elsewhere for easier pickings. If they had come by a little later, they might have decided to attack because our formation was disrupted for several minutes at the IP (Initial Point - the point where the bomb run starts). The group lead was hit by flak and lost an engine. He could not continue to lead, and signaled the deputy lead that he was leaving the formation. I was flying lead in the second element of the lead squadron and was not signaled that the group lead was leaving the formation. I, therefore, followed the lead plane until he signaled me that he was out of the formation. The deputy lead was no longer in sight. Since the whole group had accepted me as the new leader, I found myself flying as group lead. Since we were at the IP, it was simple to just get onto the bomb run, and we led the group over the target and bombed Berlin.

The flak over Berlin was intense and super accurate. The group lead was the only plane we lost, but the eighth Air Force suffered many losses. It was a real thrill to take over and lead the whole group on the bomb run and over the target. These missions are now being flown by almost a thousand bombers. What a comparison to the missions flown at the start of the year! Then we were lucky to put up a few hundred bombers.

## MISSION NUMBER 28: METZ, FRANCE
MAY 25, 1944
BOMBERS LOST: 6

This was a very easy mission. There were no fighters, and excepting the coastal batteries, flak was light and not very accurate. We almost never see enemy fighters near the coast. We bombed the marshalling yards at Metz. Marshalling yards are the complex of rail road tracks which are used to redirect trains to any particular section. Without them, it is impossible to re-route trains. This creates major problems for the military, since it becomes very difficult to supply their combat troops, or even move them from one area to another.

## MISSION NUMBER 29: LUDWIGSHAVEN, GERMANY
MAY 27, 1944
BOMBERS LOST: 32

At briefing, this mission looked as though it would be a milk run. The route to the target ran south through France and then turned a dog leg into Germany. Fighter attacks in France had fallen away off from what they had been only a few months ago. It was expected to be an easy mission since we were to have fighter escort all the way to the target and return. Our escort would be the new P-51s for the last hour and a half to the target. We were very complacent considering what we were doing.

The mission proceeded very quietly, and excepting the coastal batteries, flak was light and inaccurate. We had gotten a few minutes off schedule and this caused us to miss contact with our P-51 escort. Because of the speed at which we traveled, a few minutes translates into dozens of miles. When our last escort fighters turned and left the formation and their relief did not show up, it caused us concern, but not fright.

The entry of the P-51 into combat had resulted in severe losses to the Lufftwaffe. As a result of this, they had changed their strategy from attack regardless of the presence of escort fighters, to one in which they attacked only those formations that were without escort. To implement this program, the Lufftwaffe had inaugurated a procedure of placing one of their fighters up at 30,000 or 40,000 feet to spot for formations of bombers without escorting fighters. When they had spotted such a formation, they radioed to fighters who had been waiting. They could attack knowing our altitude, speed and direction. When such a fighter attack occurs, it is totally without warning. At the distance from which they start their attack, they are almost invisible. The rate of closure in an attack from head on is about 800 miles an hour. From the time you first see them, until they pass your plane, about fifteen or twenty seconds elapse.

About ten minutes after our last escort fighters had left, the attack started. We were still about an hour and a half from the target, when without warning; we were attacked from head on. It was still quite peaceful when Wes Creech, the top turret gunner swung his guns to face forward, firing both guns, and called "fighters 12:00 O'clock level, coming in." His guns when leveled are about twelve inches above my head. The shock of the noise of his guns and the immediate firing of all thirteen guns on the ship startled the hell out of me. I was leading the high squadron and took a fast look to see what was happening. I was startled to see about one hundred enemy planes on attack. They attacked from all angles, but the heaviest attacks were head on right through the formation.

It was difficult to differentiate between attacks because it was really a continuous stream of attacking fighters. At one point I could see that an element of three fighters was queuing up on our ship (they try to knock down a leader, since this disrupts the formation and breaks up the concentration of fire power). When I saw the fighters fire their cannons, I pulled up about fifteen feet. To do more, would make it impossible for the ships in the rear of the formation to stay in position. Tony Wagner, our bombardier, later reported seeing about a dozen twenty millimeter cannon shells explode directly beneath our ship.

This particular flight of three which had us in their sights, paid dearly for their attack. As they came in, Tony Wagner, bombardier, Wes Creech, top turret and Sam Bell in the ball turret all zeroed in on the lead fighter and blew him up as he approached. The explosion blew his right wing man into the line of fire of Marty Strom's (Navigator) gun. Marty very promptly shot his tail off. I mean this literally. It looked like a sewing machine punching holes in a sheet of paper. The tail section separated from the fuselage and both parts tumbled out of sight. As the third plane passed under us, Sam Bell and Shorty Palmer, tail gunner blasted him. Palmer reported that he had shot off the canopy and the pilot was bailing out. What actually happened was that the fighter had been crippled, and the pilot was jettisoning the canopy preparatory to bailing out. Marty Strom maintained that his was the fanciest shooting done in the Eighth Air Force. He later admitted that he was aiming for the propeller but hit the tail section.

This air battle was a disaster for the 351st Bomb Group. There were eighteen planes in the formation and seven were shot down. We were leading the high squadron and lost one plane. This was Lt. Myers, who was flying off my right wing and who for a change, was flying really good formation (Merseburg 5/12/44). Our squadron was flying excellent formation which explains why we lost only one plane. The lead squadron and the low squadron each lost three planes. Most surviving planes had been shot up severely and some were lucky to make it back to Polebrook. The most impressive of these was Lt. Anderson's plane which had a hole in the vertical stabilizer four feet by two feet. The right wing looked like a sieve where two twenty millimeter cannon shells had exploded at the rear of the number three engine. It was amazing that the ship held together and made it back to England.

As we approached the IP (Initial Point), the fighters broke off and we encountered a severe flak barrage as we went down the bomb run. After dropping our bombs and starting for home, the fighters that had been attacking us were waiting to rejoin the fight. Just as they got organized and were starting to attack, a flight of P-51s appeared and chased the German fighters off.

The above describes the attack as I saw it. I could not see the greater part of the battle, most of it happens so quickly it is impossible to describe. During this battle, I thought this was the end. I could not see any way that we could survive. In my position as leader of the high squadron, I could see the planes of the other two squadrons being shot out of the sky, one after the other. It seemed to be only a matter of minutes before it would be our turn. Our excellent formation helped to protect us and divert the German attention to the two other squadrons.

I can only describe the action I saw. There was terrific action toward the rear of the plane. I could hear the thunderous roar of the machine guns and the whole plane vibrates and shakes so severely that you wonder if it will hold together. This was without doubt the longest two hours I ever experienced. I thought it would never end. In previous scary battles, I had prayed, saying a few Hail Mary's and Our Fathers, but this was different. I did not recite orthodox prayers, I talked to God. I made bargains with Him. As things looked more and more hopeless, I kept upping the ante. At one point I said: "If you can't do it for that, forget the whole deal."

It was a miracle that we survived. Aside from divine intervention, (in which the Germans may have been praying to the same God, I think), our excellent formation and the accurate shooting of the gunners helped us through.

With respect to the quality of our squadron's formation flying, Lt. Alwyn I Keese, who was flying in my squadron, commented that our formation was so tight that if you got out of formation even a little bit you would find yourself in prop wash. He attributed our success to the good formation we were flying.

We had a relatively quiet flight back to England, and although we were shot at by the flak gunners at the coast, these seemed tame after our recent escape.

After we had landed at Polebrook, taxied to our hard top, and shut the engines down, (as I had done hundreds of times before), I dropped out of the nose hatch, and when I landed, my knees almost buckled. They didn't, and I avoided a tumble, but then standing on solid ground, I got the shakes. They lasted fifteen or twenty minutes, when they receded. After a rough mission, all combat crews are offered a double shot of scotch. I usually gave my drink to someone else because I don't like scotch. This time I thought it might be in order to accept it. I took it straight and tossed it down in one swallow. When it hit my stomach, which was still shaky, I almost threw up. It was touch and go for a few minutes. Remember we had not had anything to eat for sixteen hours. After a while, we were able to function normally, completed our review with the ground crew and went into de-briefing.

In thinking about this mission in retrospect, we realized that most of the crews that were shot down were experienced crews. Several of these crews were flying missions in the "gray zone" (the extra five missions over twenty five). These were men that we knew and would miss. On most missions, it is the new crews that get shot down—people that we never had the time or opportunity to get to know.

*James J. "Reddo" Redmond, Jr.*

Our surviving this mission in the face of such overwhelming odds is a tribute to my crew.  Their performance in such terrifying conditions and circumstances is a tribute to their loyalty and their confidence in each other.  Without these, I am not at all certain that we would have survived the day.

As we went to de-briefing, the thought occurred to me that perhaps the violent reactions I experienced were the cumulative effects of having flown 29 missions.  Certainly we were beyond the threshold which the Air Force had determined a combat crewman should not exceed.

The formation diagram on the following page shows the 351st Bomb Group formation as it left England on the mission to Ludwigshaven on May 27, 1944.  This diagram is an exact reproduction of the diagram distributed to the Aircraft Commanders at briefing.  Those planes which were shot down have been shaded with an "X."

## Group Formation

Combat Flight Leader: Lt. Dixey
Deputy Flight Leader: Lt. Kogelman
Date: 5/27/44

(Ludwigshaven, Germany)

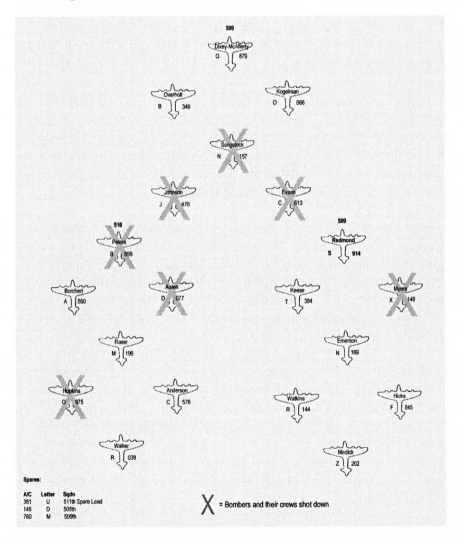

Spares:

| A/C | Letter | Sqdn |
|-----|--------|------|
| 381 | U | 511th Spare Lead |
| 146 | D | 508th |
| 760 | M | 509th |

X = Bombers and their crews shot down

*James J. "Reddo" Redmond, Jr.*

## MISSION NUMBER 30: CAEN, FRANCE ("D" DAY)
JUNE 6, 1944
BOMBERS LOST: 6

This is to be our thirtieth mission. Our last mission. The goal of flying thirty missions had seemed to be almost unattainable, but it looks as though we will make it. There remained a nagging fear that something would go wrong, and you would get shot down. This had happened to a number of crews, but then it always happens to somebody else.

When we entered the briefing room there seemed to be something different. The air was electric. Then the room was secured and the map was unveiled. Then we knew. This was to be "D" Day. The feeling among the combat crews was concern for those poor bastards hitting the beach. I think every one of the combat crew men said a mental prayer for them.

Joe Berardi (a fellow Aircraft commander) and I, were both flying our last mission. In accordance with tradition, we would buzz the tower when we returned. It was a first that two crews would finish their tour on the same mission. We made plans that we would buzz in formation. This would be a first. Then we realized that this was too serious a day for us to play and we called off our performance.

The actual mission was not very exciting. There was cloud cover blocking any view of the channel and the invasion beaches. We had been looking forward to seeing the vast armada of the invasion fleet and the assault on the beaches. There were no enemy fighters and flak was light and not very accurate. The mission was an early one and we were back about lunch time. It was announced that there would be a second mission that afternoon, and we would have to fly it. It was also announced that since the invasion had begun, there would be no tour limits. We had not completed our tour. We would be required to continue flying indefinitely. The weather deteriorated and the second mission was not flown.

## MISSION NUMBER 31: BERNAY ST. MARTIN, FRANCE
JUNE 11, 1944
BOMBERS LOST: 5

Flying this mission was anti-climactic. The enthusiasm experienced in all the previous missions was not there. We encountered no enemy fighters and received very little flak. The bombing was done through clouds so we could not even see how accurate we were. There were no losses, and very little damage to the planes.

The only ever-present concern was the fear that something would go wrong. Like Murphy's Law, "If anything can go wrong, it will go wrong."

## MISSION NUMBER 32: CAMBRAI, FRANCE
JUNE 12, 1944
BOMBERS LOST: 17

There were no fighters encountered and only light flak. The flak, however, was very accurate and shot one plane down. The plane, although severely damaged, was able to make it to the channel where they ditched (ditch is a crash landing in water). Two of the crew died either from drowning or exposure. The other eight were picked up by Air-Sea Rescue and survived. Most of the planes suffered considerable damage.

## MISSION NUMBER 33: PARIS, FRANCE
JUNE 14, 1944
BOMBERS LOST: 19

This mission was to Le Bourget Air Field. (This was the field that Lindberg had landed at in 1927.) Bombing results were good with much damage to hangers and work shops. About forty to fifty enemy planes approached, but decided not to attack, probably because we were flying good formation. I guess they decided to look for easier prey. We learned a long time ago how important it was to fly good formation.

Flak was very heavy both at the target and at Dieppe on the coast. Three planes were shot down. One was the group lead flown by a very experienced crew. The pilot's name was Joe Dixie. He was directly in front of me as he left the formation and blew into one of those brilliant red /orange flashes from which are left only scraps. The other two ships that went down were flown by new crews. I did not know them.

One plane, piloted by Lt Raser, a friend of mine, was a victim of flak at the target. He had just dropped his bombs when a 155 mm shell burst immediately below the open bomb bay doors. Damage was extensive. The plane was riddled with holes, two engines on the same wing were knocked out, and some of the control cables were severed. This, with the uneven thrust of the two engines, made the plane almost impossible to control. However, Raser was able to maintain some control of the plane by use of the auto pilot and the remaining controls. Once out of the formation, Raser had to put the plane in a gentle glide to maintain flying speed. Meanwhile, the engineer had cut pieces of wire off the trailing antenna, and using these pieces was able to connect enough of the broken control wires to give Raser almost full control of the plane. Raser made it to England where he landed at an emergency field. His landing was delayed to allow another plane to land ahead of him. That plane was on fire.

An amusing thing was observed. All that saw it thought it was funny. An American fighter had caught a German training plane alone over Paris, and decided to shoot it down. The training plane had a top speed of probably 120 miles an hour. The American fighter's speed was over 400 miles an hour. The German plane headed for the Eiffel Tower and was circling it so the American could not get a good shot at him. The last I saw of this, the German was still circling the tower, and the American was still trying to get a shot at him.

An after the war note: I saw no parachutes exit from Joe Dixie's plane. I was convinced that all ten crew members had perished in the explosion. I carried this recollection until June 2001, when at the 351st reunion in San Diego, I was waiting for the tour bus when I noticed the name tag on a gentleman that read "Joe Dixie". I was startled and asked him if he hadn't been blown up in combat, as I recalled. He replied that yes his plane had been blown up but they escaped seconds before the explosion, and had spent the balance of the war as a POW (prisoner of war).

## MISSION NUMBER 34: HAMBURG, GERMANY
JUNE 20, 1944
BOMBERS LOST: 50

This was a very early morning mission and we were not too eager to go. There was a nagging sensation that something might go wrong. We all thought we were running on borrowed time. However, as always, we got ready and went on the mission. We saw only a few enemy fighters which were quickly chased away by our P-47 escort. The flak at the target was extremely intense and very accurate. Most planes in our group suffered substantial damage, although we lost no planes. The Eighth Air Force lost about fifty planes today.

The number of planes on these missions has increased so dramatically to missions with about a thousand planes compared to the missions of only a few months ago when a maximum effort meant a couple hundred planes. Replacement crews are poring in so fast that there is no time to get to know them. Fighter attacks and pitched air battles are fast becoming a thing of the past. The most danger to the bombers is now from flak which is becoming more intense and accurate.

Even though Hamburg is a good distance from England, we got back at lunch time because of the early start. During lunch it was announced that there would be another mission that afternoon. I

143

was still hyped up with the adrenaline flowing and I thought that I could handle another mission. I was hopeful that the mission tour would be set at thirty-five, and if so, we could complete our tour that day. I spoke to the crew to see if they were agreeable to this. As usual, they would do whatever I suggested. Then fatigue began to set in and I was sorry I had volunteered. While I was thinking of a way to get out of flying that afternoon, it was announced that anyone who had thirty missions on "D" Day had completed their tour.

I didn't know how to feel. It had been such an up and down day. First flying a mission, then volunteering for the afternoon mission; then trying to think of a way out of it; then hearing the announcement that meant I was finished.

It seemed too good to be true. I had achieved the goal I had been seeking since I began flying. The sensation of satisfaction was tainted with a sense of loss of something. I was no longer a combat crew man. I would no longer share their apprehension and anxieties about combat missions. The combat crew men offered their envious congratulations, but there was a barrier that had never existed before. It was obvious that I was no longer one of them.

Previously, my life had changed from the safety of non combat to the mortal dangers of combat. Now it would be changed back. Already I could feel the loss of the excitement of combat, and wondered what would fill this void. I, and some others who had completed their tour, did some sight seeing. Nothing seemed to compensate for the thrill of combat. After a few weeks of nothing to do, orders came through directing me back to the States. This was a new venture and I seized upon it as a remedy for my feeling of lack of completeness. As new situations arose they tended to substitute for those sensations engendered by combat but I doubt that anything will replace the thrill and excitement of combat, or completely eradicate them.

# OBSERVATIONS ABOUT COMBAT

Many times in my descriptions of our combat tour, I commented that a mission was a "milk run" and only a handful of planes were damaged or lost.  This was true for us, the survivors, but consider the situation where a single plane is hit by either flak or fighters, and there are wounded or dead on board, or the plane has been destroyed.  Visualize the terror experienced by that crew as they face death with no alternative.  For them this was hell.  Regardless of the successes of the Eighth Air Force, this was not a "milk run" at all.

The question of grief as the result of the loss of friends in combat is frequently raised.  In my opinion, grief was not a significant factor in the day to day lives of the combat crew man.  A possible explanation, and one which was true for me, was that there were relatively few close relationships formed between crews.  Very few crews completed their tour since most were shot down in combat.  The statistic of two out of three combat crew men being KIA (killed in action) mitigated against formation of any close friendship.  The crew man you were friendly with today, might be killed on tomorrow's mission.  Not only did it make more sense to avoid a close relationship, but the length of time available for creating such a relationship was limited by the casualties.  This absence of closeness substantially reduced any grief experienced by surviving combat crew men.  This was expressed by the combat crew man's philosophy "Better he than me."

The exception to this lack of comradeship applied totally to members of your crew, where a loss would be catastrophic and to a lesser degree, to pilots with whom you were close friends as cadets.

145

# CORRESPONDENCE

This series of letters between me, Jim Redmond, better known as "Reddo," the Aircraft Commander and Lloyd W. Bogle, the Radio operator of the combat crew known as "Reddo's Raiders," constitute this section identified as Correspondence. This series of letters started in April 1998 and continued to October 1999. Each letter raises some aspect of the combat missions participated in or some occurrence involving the crew and the subsequent letter responds to this and raises new items. The flow continues until most of those memorable items of our combat days have been discussed to the best of our memories.

The letters are presented here in a basically unaltered form. The grammar and punctuation may not be correct, but to correct such errors might change the intent of the written word. Therefore they are presented as they were written.

# LETTER NUMBER 1
APRIL 29, 1998

Pilot to Radio, where have you been all this time?

I have been reading the Polebrook Post for years looking for the name of any of my old crew then just yesterday there it was, Lloyd Bogle, Radio Operator of "Reddo's Raiders."

Believe me it was a thrill, I tried a couple of times to locate all the members of our crew but got no response from any of them.

I did see Sam Bell in St. Louis ages ago. Probably 40 years ago. I was on a business trip that took me through St. Louis and I was able to contact Sam (Ball Turret). We had a nice visit and he drove me to the airport. I've tried his old address since but no response. I tried Marty Strom (Navigator), Frank Cavanaugh (Co-Pilot), Tony Wagner (Bombardier), Wes Creech (Engineer-Top Turret), Pop Beyer (Waist Gunner), Vern Palmer (Tail Gunner), Jack Vinson (Waist Gunner). No response from any of them.

By now I suppose some of them are dead. That's something the Germans could not do to us. We had exchanged letters a couple of times but I lost your address.

I know a very good friend of mine Lowry Brisby looked you up and visited with you, but that also was a long time ago. He is dead now too but he told me how he enjoyed speaking with you.

If you have any contact with any of our crew let me know. It is a shame to lose all contact when we were so close in training and in combat.

*James J. "Reddo" Redmond, Jr.*

Several of your comments still remain in memory. Once during one of our missions everybody was firing at enemy fighters and the plane was shaking all over the place. The intercom was in an uproar and you could not see any fighters through your window. You made the announcement that since you could not help, you were going to hide under the radio table.

I also remember the time you forgot to get me my pilot's radio flimsy. (This would have left me incommunicado with the rest of the formation) You had to leave the plane at "start engines" and run back to the radio shack. You just made it back. We were next for take off. You remember this delayed your promotion to tech sgt for about two months.

I remain in excellent health and still work even though I will be 78 years old next August.

If you've got time and don't forget, drop me a line and bring me up to date.

Do you remember Bogle's secret weapon that scared the crap out of Palmer? The flotation rafts were stored on the side of the fuselage and were to be released by a handle in the radio room. You, moving around with your gun, hooked the release handle with your parachute harness and popped the raft loose during a gun fight. It went past the tail position, all the time inflating, and poor Palmer though the plane was coming apart.

All for now, looking to hear from you.

Over and out.

Reddo.

# LETTER NUMBER 2
MAY 15, 1998

Radio to Pilot:

It gave me quite a thrill to hear from my old pilot and to know that your health is still in good shape. I regret to hear your good friend Brisby passed away some time ago. We had a good time talking about many things.

I'm sorry to say that I don't know anything about any of the rest of the crew members. I have thought of them often and wondered if they are still alive.

This is the second time I have subscribed for the Polebrook Post. The first time it went defunct or I quit getting the Post. Just recently I received a letter from the editor asking for new members and I subscribed again. On the first edition I received my name wasn't on the roster. Your name was the only name of crew on the roster. I was looking forward to communicating with them. My name appeared in the last edition but they made one small mistake. It should be Lloyd W. Bogle, not Lloyd B. Bogle.

It's really great to know you still remember some of the events that happened so many years ago. I still remember them vividly.

Wonder if you remember this one. Before we ever flew a mission, we were all in our combat gear, ready to get on board our plane for our first mission, and you said you wanted our attention. Your words were very forceful. "If there is any man in my crew that thinks he is not going to make it through this, all the missions we have to fly, I want you to speak up now. If you have a feeling you won't make it, I want you to say so now. (of course nobody said anything) Then you said that if anyone had that feeling you would see to it that whoever felt that way would be transferred to another crew. You then said "This crew is going to complete their twenty five mission without a loss, so lets go see what this as all about."

Did you know that Vinson (Waist gunner) never fired a shot over enemy territory? He would freeze with fear. But Beyer (Waist Gunner) said he could handle both positions. So you believed Beyers and kept Vinson on the crew. This is fantastic flying thirty five missions and never firing a shot over enemy territory because of fear. You know this as I do. You don't know what you're made of until you're tested. I think you had ten good men that would have gone to hell and back as long as you were at the helm in the pilot's seat.

I want to tell you this before I close. I might have told you before. After I received my discharge I went to Lubbock Texas where my wife was going to college to get her degree. I started work at South Plains Air Force Base putting B-17s in moth balls. Pickling them as we called it. I was always on the lookout for Triangle J aircraft and one day I spotted one. As I got closer I could see very clearly written on the nose of the plane, "MY PRINCESS." I was so thrilled as I entered the aircraft. It was as if I was taken back into the past. When I walked up to the radio desk where I had sat for so many missions I saw the inscription I had carved into the desk with a pocket knife. It was the only scripture I could remember. "Even though I walk through the valley of the shadow of death, I will fear no evil, for thou art with me. Thy rod and Thy staff, they comfort me,"

It was so nice to hear from you, Reddo, please let me hear from you again.

I have an electric typewriter but I'm not much better with it than I am with pen.

Radio to pilot, over and out.

150

## LETTER NUMBER 3
MAY 23, 1998

Dear Lloyd:

I was really glad to get your letter. It brought back a lot of memories. I really remember that little talk I gave just before our first mission. I was probably just as nervous as any of you, but I thought I'd better try to put the rest of you as much at as ease as possible. I was sort of surprised that you remembered it so well. I really did not expect anyone to say he wanted out. I'm not sure what I could have done if any one had. Anyway, I guess it had the desired effect.

About Vinson not firing his gun over enemy territory. This took a little thought but I finally reconstructed the situation. The entire crew, minus Vinson, approached me with the disclosure that Vinson was too terrified to fire his gun in combat. They had obviously given this matter considerable thought, and wanted me to be aware of the situation. They said that if I wanted to replace Vinson they would be agreeable. They felt however that they could handle his gun. Fighter attacks seldom came from both sides at the same time, and Beyer our thirty-odd year old waist gunner said he could handle both guns. Our crew was such a cohesive unit that I hated to bring in a new member. I was afraid that we might be assigned a man who did not fit in with the crew. Based on this I agreed that we would continue with Vinson until such time as they thought it was endangering the crew. I don't know how Vinson could have gone on all those missions so scared that he couldn't fire a gun. Anyway no one outside our crew ever knew of this situation.

Kind of on that subject did you know that Pop Beyer came to me when we received our shipping orders to go overseas and told me that he wanted out, off the crew? I was flabbergasted and more than a little mad. We sat in my car and talked about it. His explanations and reasons didn't seem to make sense. I was having a hard time controlling my temper. I was so pissed off that he would continue training with the crew and at the last minute say he wanted off the crew. Finally after about two hours Beyer leveled with me and said the reason he wanted off the crew was that he was afraid that when we got overseas they would ground him because of his age. I explained to him that we had trained for four months to become a team that would become a combat crew. No one would break up that crew. I told him that I would not let anyone remove a member of our crew. He asked if I could guarantee him that. I said yes I could. Beyer smiled and said to forget everything he said before. He wanted to stay on the crew. That was the last time this matter was ever discussed.

About Beyer and his age (advanced years). As I recall he was in mid-thirties. I thought he would be a stabilizing influence on the crew. Was I wrong, he was as ready for nonsense as any one on the crew.

You may remember that Beyer was the last member to join the crew. There was a vacancy at waist gunner created by Jack Ward's being accepted for Aviation Cadet training. Headquarters furnished me with the name of a man to replace Ward. I gave the man's name to you five remaining crew men, and suggested that you look him up and see what you think of him. After about an hour the five of you reported that you did not want him on the crew. I recommended that you give him a chance. Again you reported that you did not want him on the crew. The crew felt that he would disrupt the crew. This was enough for me. I went to headquarters and requested a different candidate. Headquarters really gave me a hard time saying I had no choice. When things got to this level, I suggested we check with the C.O. This changed the picture, and they came up with Beyer's name. As I did before, I gave Beyer's name to the crew and told them to look him up. The next thing I knew the crew reported arm in arm with Beyer to introduce him as the new member of the crew.

All in all, Lloyd, I think we had the best and finest combat crew in any Air Force, especially the Mighty Eighth. I may be prejudiced, but I stand by that.

I have a lot of recollections to share with you as we correspond. I don't know about you but I sometimes get Goosebumps when I think about these things. This was a great experience for those of us who were lucky enough to live through it; Never to be forgotten! But let's face it, in a few years there will be none of us left. As far as history is concerned I saw a school history book last week. World War 2 was covered in two pages. The Mighty Eighth was not mentioned at all.

I guess it will be up to us to keep the memory of "Reddo's Raiders" alive.

Let's not drop contact again. Keep healthy and happy.
Reddo.

*James J. "Reddo" Redmond, Jr.*

# LETTER NUMBER 4
JUNE 6, 1998

Dear Reddo;

I'll try this letter again in longhand. I was never much of a penman, but I'm not much of a typist either. I have a good electric typewriter, but I can't type very fast, so I thought I'd try again with my pen.

I apologize for being so long in answering your most welcome letter. I've read it several times, in fact, I just got through reading it again. I never get tired reading about things that happened when I was a member of "Reddo's Raiders" combat crew. My mind wonders about the rest of the crew occasionally, wondering if they are still living. I remember what each state each crew member came from except the co-pilot, Cavanaugh. Do you remember on one of our missions we took a piece of flak through the cockpit and it cut Cavanaugh's parachute off him and I heard you later say that the cockpit was so full of feathers that it was hard to see the instrument panel. I'm sure this still registers plainly in your mind. It was easy to tell when we got hit, whether it was flak or German fighters. It could be heard from one of the plane to the other.

I'll never forget one mission we were on. You no doubt remember it. It was Manheim on the east bank of the Rhine. Aachen was on the west bank of the Rhine. We had to fight all the way in and all the way out. We fought the German fighters all the way in to the I.P. (initial point.- The spot where the bomb run is commenced). As we left the target and got out of the range of the flak guns, the Lufftwaffe attacked again. I saw more B-17s go down on this mission than on any other. The 509th Squadron alone had put up a maximum effort of thirteen B-17s I saw two

German fighters attack the squadron flying off our left wing. They came in from three o'clock high. They were out of range for our fifty caliber guns to do any good. One of the German fighters hit the right wing of a B-17 and bounced off in flames and then exploded. The other fighter kept going straight down. The impact knocked a wing off the B-17 and set it on fire sending out of control in a spinning motion and on fire. I watched it until it was out of sight. I never saw any chutes come from the plane. My stomach felt about the size of my fist right up in my throat. I was never so glad to see the English Channel. This is only one of many missions that "Reddo's Raiders" were on, but I think this to be the bloodiest.

Oh! by the way, when I forgot the flimsy I wouldn't have made it back in time if it hadn't been for a jeep driver that brought me back to the plane, breaking the speed limit all the way. I just made it. You were taxiing into position for take off when I came on board.

Since I have subscribed to the Polebrook Post, I have heard from an associate in England. There are several of them that are still interested in keeping alive what the Eighth Air Force accomplished while we were there. He wants some first hand history on the actual details as they took place. His grandchildren use them in their history lessons. It's another way of keeping the Eighth Air Force alive, I intend to respond. Another guy I served with in the Elution Islands (I served two hitches in the Air Force). He wants to hear from me. Intend to do just that.

I apologize for waiting as long as I did to write you. The Lord knows I really enjoy your letters.

Let me hear from you regularly. Keep yourself in good shape and health.

Lloyd

*James J. "Reddo" Redmond, Jr.*

# LETTER NUMBER 5
JULY 4, 1998

Dear Lloyd:

Frank Cavanaugh was from Boston, Mass. I tried to contact him some time ago, but got no response.

You mentioned the raid on Manheim. Would you believe I don't remember this mission? This is probably because I would not be aware of action taking place at the waist or tail positions except as I would pick it up through the intercom. I am sure I was aware of it but not the intensity that existed.

The worst mission that I recall was the one to Ludswigshaven. This took place during the last few days of May 1944. Here again we had to fight our way to the target, bomb, and fight our way out. On this mission we were leading the high squadron and we lost our right wing man. The pilot was a guy named Meyers. He was the worst formation flyer I ever saw but this day he was really flying good formation (possibly because I was on his back about it). Nevertheless he was shot down. During that mission the 509th lost just that one but the lead squadron lost its whole second element, three planes, and the low squadron lost three planes. A total of seven planes out of the eighteen planes of the 351st Bomb Group. Lt. Alwyn Keese who was on our left wing said after we returned that I flew the squadron in so tight that if he got even a little bit out of position he would find himself in prop wash. He acknowledged that the tight formation probably accounted for our loss of only one plane.

You may remember that we claimed three fighters destroyed. I saw this because the attack came head on. I saw the lead fighter blow up about three or four hundred yards in front of us and the explosion blew his right wing man into the line of fire of Marty Strom's gun, whereupon Strom proceeded to shoot the tail off the German fighter. For a while Strom claimed this to be the fanciest shooting done by anyone in the Eighth Air Force. He said that anyone can shoot a plane down but it takes talent to shoot their tails off. One night in the Combat Officer's club, after about a dozen beers, he admitted he was shooting for the propeller.

Perhaps you will remember this one. On about our thirteenth mission "My Princess" was laid up for battle damage and we were flying a plane that did not have Tokyo tanks. On the way to the target we were hit by flak and our number four engine was knocked out and set on fire. I got the fire out and feathered the prop. Then number one engine was hit. I don't remember what the damage was, but the engine would run, but not pull much power. I did not feather the prop but kept the engine running at idle so that if things got worse I could bring it back and maybe get some use out of it. In the meantime we were out of the formation and going it alone. We were inspected by three Me 109s but I was able to contact some American fighters and as soon as they appeared the enemy fighters beat it. The American fighters escorted us to the coast. Now the part of this that I want to get to is this.

Since we were in trouble, you, along with the rest of the crew, were trying to be on top of everything in your area. The controls for transfer of fuel from Tokyo tanks to the main tanks were located in the bomb bay. It would be your job to make a transfer when I asked you to. You were aware that fuel might be a problem and decided to look in the bomb bay and locate the controls so that there would be no delay when I asked you to transfer. You could not find any controls because there were none. You reported this to me, and knowing that this plane did not have Tokyo tanks, I told you not to worry about it. I would tell you where the controls were when I needed them. This did not satisfy you and you called again to report that you still could not find the controls. I tried to placate you but not too successfully.

157

Sam Bell in the ball turret now piped in to tell me that he was sure that there were no Tokyo tanks because he had checked on this before we took off. You probably remember that Sam was a graduate engineer and regularly checked everything. Now the entire crew knew that we did not have Tokyo tanks and surmised that fuel would be a problem. The whole crew began to bitch and complain that we never should have gone on the mission, that it was our thirteenth, etc. etc. etc. I got the crew settled down and directed my attention to our fuel problem, which was compounded by the fact that Cavanaugh was grounded with a cold or something and we had a substitute co-pilot. He was so scared and nervous I thought he might crap his pants. (Maybe he did, I don't know) With our high fuel consumption having only two engines and the high power settings necessary, he was all up tight and computing our fuel reserves every two minutes. It was his conclusion that we could make it back to England but he was including the fuel he thought we had in Tokyo tanks. When he found out that we did not have Tokyo tanks he became hyper.

He was sure we could not make it back to England. I knew it would be close as to making it back to Polebrook but I was confident that at worst we could land at some base near the coast in England. We made it all the way back to Polebrook. When we entered the traffic pattern and were making a turn onto the base leg the co-pilot grabbed the wheel and pulled us out of our bank. I thought we were in danger of running into something that I didn't see. I hollered what's wrong He said the turn was too steep for a plane with an engine out. By this time I was really fed up with him and told him to sit quiet and don't touch anything. Now I had to really increase our bank to make the landing. He sat there and did what he was told. After landing and debriefing I reported to operations that I never wanted that co-pilot again. We were a full hour later in returning than the group which had gone on to the target. When we walked into the interrogation room debriefing was almost over. We had been reported as missing in action and there were several eye witness reports of our having been blown up.

Oh! Incidentally, our ship, "My Princess" was supposed to be on the dust cover of the history book of the 351st. The dust cover never got made. I have the art work it was to be made from. If you would like, I can have a copy of the picture made and send it to you.

Even though "My Princess" was officially our plane, I much preferred to fly the new G models. The electronic controls on the supercharger made altitude formation flying a cinch.

Pilot to radio, over and out.

*James J. "Reddo" Redmond, Jr.*

# LETTER NUMBER 6
JULY 30, 1998

Dear Reddo:

I keep all of your letters. I don't have a filing system. (I think I misspelled that word). I think of the past missions we had together all the time.

I can remember when we went on a mission in the invasion of France in June 1944. I was so proud to go on this mission. We had been briefed that everything was a maximum effort and I wanted to see all the ships down below. As it happened it was cloud cover below us and we couldn't see a thing. As I remember you flew two or three missions that day as an extra pilot on another crew. (I think it was three) (the ball turret gunner did the same thing). I was the last of our crew to finish my missions because I developed an eye infection and had to go to the hospital because of a loose fitting oxygen mask.

I remember Ludwigshaven very well but I did not get a front view like you did. I got it in my diary. We seen so many of these types of missions. Have you ever wondered how we made it?

I remember the thirteenth mission like yesterday. Coming back from deep inside Germany, crippled and without any fighter support until you got in touch with a couple of our fighters and as you said they escorted us to the English Channel. As I remember now we couldn't find our secondary target, so we, as you well know, couldn't bring our bombs back to base so we bombed a fellows potato patch. We never received thanks for digging his potatoes. (only kidding)

Can you remember how many times we bombed Schwienfurt? I think it should be spelled Schweinfurt. I could dig up my diary but

160

it would take a little time. We hit it so many times and they kept building it back because it was a ball bearing plant and vital to the German war effort. Finally the Eighth Air Force high command sent down the order to wipe the city of Schweinfurt off the map. This we did. Do you remember this order we helped carry out? War is hell as president Roosevelt said. You and I both know that it is. You don't know what kind of stuff you're made of until your life is on the line. That's the reason that Vinson could never fire a shot over enemy territory. He froze with fear but he was willing to put his life on the line.

Reddo, I'm going to send you what I got from Frank Urbanek. He might be able to help you to locate some of the crew members. You can do what you want with it. I don't know how to go about this. I guess I'm still depending on my pilot.

I'll let you in on a little secret that I never told you before. I'm a musician and I have a band. I have played professionally for several years. I love doing it but it's more a hobby. We play for dances three to four times a month and sometimes we play for special occasions. It's a lot of fun. I'll bet you had no idea that you had a musician as radio operator on your crew. By the way I play lead guitar in a terrific country band called the "Starlighters." I'm going to send you some pictures. I'll see if I can get them in this letter, if not, the next.

The associate member of the 351st that I've been writing at Peterborough, England sent me some pictures of the base at Polebrook. They were not very good. One hanger was pretty good and the main gate. If you want them, I'll send you a copy.

Reddo, why don't you send me your phone number and I'll give you a buzz. I'd like to hear your voice again and if you have some recent snapshots of you and your family, I'd appreciate it.

From Radio to pilot, over and out.

Lloyd

*James J. "Reddo" Redmond, Jr.*

# LETTER NUMBER 7
AUGUST 13, 1998

Dear Lloyd:

Sorry to be so long in answering your last letter. I took a couple of weeks off and visited my daughter in Buffalo, N.Y. We took a short trip into the Adirondack Mountains where I had gone to camp when I was a kid.

I haven't been able to locate the picture that was used for the dust cover of the 351st book. I will continue to look and will enclose it in a future letter. Actually the dust cover was never made because of the lack of time. I am sure I have the picture that was used. It is small but you can have it blown up. I also have a picture of you which I will send when I can have it duplicated.

I never knew that you had been wounded. You never were one to keep things to himself. You probably never knew that I was also nicked. I don't remember which mission it happened on. I remember there were a great number of wounded and our little hospital was very busy. I went down to the hospital the next day to show then my "wound." Apiece of flak had come into the plane, through the floors etc. and was pretty well spent when it hit my finger. It hit the second finger left hand at the second knuckle. It was a miserable little piece, very skinny about two inches long and tapered like an arrow head. It was very jagged. I pulled it out. The wound did not bleed much only a drop or two, and dried up. My good gloves were ruined and you know how tough it was to get equipment. The flak had pushed the cartilage up in my finger and can still be felt as a small lump. There is a dark spot at the point of entry. It didn't affect the movement of the finger at all.

But back to the visit to the hospital. As I said, I went to the hospital the next day to show them. When they examined my finger, they called all the doctors and medics to examine my wound. After lots of kidding they prescribed a band aid and told me to take two aspirins and do not call them in the morning. They did not believe that I had been hit the previous day.

On another occasion a piece of flak came through the bottom of the plane, through the navigator's floor, through my floor, and hit me on the bottom of my boot. Fortunately it was spent by that time and had only enough zip to knock my foot off the ruder pedal. However I thought I was hit and since this happened on the bomb run no matter what, I couldn't check on it. During the time it took to complete the bomb run about four or five minutes, I went through all the emotions of being wounded. My feet were so cold that there was not much feeling in them. My foot didn't seem to hurt and I attributed this to shock. I wondered how long it would be before it started to hurt. This was of real concern because the trip back would take four or five hours. When the bombs were dropped I could loosen up the formation and turn the plane over to Cavanaugh and examine my foot. The flak had scooped out a section of the boot. I found this piece of flak too and saved it for a long time but both have been lost.

I am enclosing a list of missions, target, date, etc. that Lt. Van Tassel, Ass't operations officer of the squadron made for me. You remember Van Tassel don't you? He got the piss scared out of him on his first mission and got relieved of combat. He served as Ass't operations officer until the missions got easy after "D" day when he got back on combat status. He sat out the rough ones and flew when it got easy.

You really surprised me to find out you were a musician. I can't figure out why you kept this a secret from the crew. We could have had you play and sing us a lullaby when things were tough.

Do you remember all the candy we bought on the way over? As I remember we bought about fifteen cases of candy which was to last us all through our tour. It took about a month to get to England and when we were settled I discovered that you gunners had eaten every last bar of candy. We were right. Candy was in short supply. We had about twenty cases of fruit juice which we had been hoarding, and when we got to Polebrook we found there was no shortage of fruit juices.

On our flight over the Atlantic, do you remember that just at sunrise I thought I saw a ship on fire? We started to steer toward it but were not getting any closer. I asked Marty Strom our navigator to estimate its position so we could send as SOS. You had the radio all set to start broadcasting when Strom broke in on the interphone and hollered don't send anything. That's the Morning Star "Venus." This was like nothing I had seen before or since.

Anyway Lloyd, I'll send those pics, probably next letter.

Pilot to radio, over and out.

# LETTER NUMBER 8
SEPTEMBER 3, 1998

Dear Reddo:

I don't remember you getting hit by flak, in fact, twice, but only tore a hole in your boot which was enough to make you think it was serious. Did you get the Purple Heart for the injury to your finger? I laughed at what they told you at the hospital, "put a bandage on it and take two aspirins". That was funny. You saved the piece of flak that took out part of the sole of your boot. Well I never did tell you this but on one of our missions I had been looking out the radio window and for some unknown reason I moved my head back away from the window and then suddenly this piece of flak came smashing through the window and lodged in the fuselage above my head just sticking into the fuselage. I pried it out and carried it as a souvenir for a long time until it got lost.

I can't remember the candy or the juice we took with us but I can remember the 5th of scotch whiskey or some other brand that you brought along to celebrate Christmas. That was a joyous occasion and the crew didn't know you had it until you broke it out on Christmas Day.

Reddo, I don't know whether it is worth mentioning or not but the only way to know is to ask. I always admired you and looked up to you to bring us through. I thought you were something close to steel. What I am trying to say, after going through so much stress and strain did you ever fly any combat missions in your dreams after you had completed your tour of duty? I will tell you the truth, I have flown several, and just as real as what you and I flew. I guess you call it combat fatigue. All that is gone, just the true experiences are left with me and I wouldn't take anything for them.

Yes I remember the ball of fire you seen, and I was almost on the verge of sending an SOS and Strom stopped me. I didn't see the star myself but would liked to have seen it. Could it have been something supernatural?

There's lots of things to talk about but I'll sign off now and talk about them next time.

Radio to pilot, over and out.

# LETTER NUMBER 9
SEPTEMBER 7, 1998

Dear Lloyd:

Before I forget it, I am also keeping copies of our letters. I did not make a copy of my first letter to you. Will you please make a copy of it and send it to me?

No, I never got the Purple Heart for my finger wound. After my visit to the medics, I was too embarrassed to even talk about it. It is only recently that I have even talked about it.

I have a bunch of pictures to enclose with this letter. One pic is of that B-17 that I crash landed at Elizabeth, Louisiana. You guys bailed out, and the co-pilot and I crash landed the plane. The next day I had to report to the C.O. who asked me what the plane was good for now. The only reply I could think of was "spare parts". This of course pissed him off completely Actually the real reason for the crash was that the plane had not been properly serviced before we took it up. They were glad to get a hold of me, because I was the first pilot they could talk to out of five fatal crashes during the previous two weeks.

As I remember, you had some back injury as a result of your landing. How do you feel now? According to my recollection, all the crew became celebrities in Elizabeth, La. I did not get a chance to cash in on this because I could not leave the base until they finished the crash investigation. We were about to leave for overseas and it was too late to participate. I felt bad about this because I had been able to communicate in a nice way with what I thought was the prettiest one of the girls in Elizabeth.

*James J. "Reddo" Redmond, Jr.*

Most of the pictures were taken after one of our missions. From the expressions, it must have been one of the easy ones.

In one picture you seem to be explaining the length of something.  I don't know what it was, but I suspect you are exaggerating.  Maybe it had something to do with the House of the Seven Virgins.  Ask your wife what she thinks.  Some of the pictures were taken at Southport where we went on flak leave. That little boy who you have your hand on was not really your son, was he?

I am enclosing a copy of my recollections of our missions taken from a brief diary of my impressions of our missions.  Actually I am enclosing two copies.  Please take one of them and mark any additions and corrections and send it back to me.

I hope I am not asking too much of you, but I would like to have as accurate a history of our crew as possible.

Well, I guess I have given you enough to keep you out of mischief for a while.

Yes, I would like very much to have pictures of your family and the band.

Over and out,
Reddo.

# LETTER NUMBER 10
SEPTEMBER 25, 1998

Dear Reddo:

I choose nights when everything is quiet and I can concentrate.

It was so good to hear your voice, it was so clear, almost like you were talking to me face to face. It has been fifty four years and the ties that bind are just as strong now as they were then. I consider you still my pilot as it was then. I think destiny has bound us together, (I keep having to change pens, I guess you noticed)

I'm working on what you want and I'll get it to you.

I'm worried about your safety because of the hurricane Georges. We've been watching it and they talk about their concern for Ft. Lauderdale as well as southern Florida.

Reddo, I've put all the things I could think of in all of your missions report. I've got to be honest, Reddo, according to my diary, Wilhemshaven was our first mission and our third was Leipzig, but I don't want to change your report because it included all the missions and it was such a good detailed description of the missions. It was so good I could think back to the way it was then.

I don't want to change anything because everything is in there. Everything is good but I can't find Manheim. I was on a lot of rough ones but to me this one was a little bit rougher than Ludwigshaven because I seen so many B-17s go down in flame. You have written a good account of our missions. I was thrilled that you take that much interest in the war. I would like to see your account of what happened published. You have a gift of describing the way things happened.

169

*James J. "Reddo" Redmond, Jr.*


There was more than one occasion that I thought I would probably never get back to Polebrook again. You might not believe this but I always thought that because we had a good pilot somehow we would get back and get through it all. You must have had a rabbit's foot in your pocket. I don't believe this either. If you really want to know what I think, that the Lord was with us. Have you ever counted The B-17s that went down during the time we were flying our missions, and how the odds were stacked against us, yet we made it, and as far as I know, only You and I were injured, but only minor.

My band and I made music tonight for a dance and had a good crowd. Everything went well, lots of compliments and this goes when you play well. I will get some recent pictures made of the band when we're playing. I'm going to send you some which are close to being up to date.

I haven't asked you what you do with your free time, or your hobby. You don't have to feel you have to answer, but my hobby or pastime is music. I've been involved with it on and off all my life. I make a little extra money out of it.

You flew thirty four missions, I flew thirty three. You wound up as a major. I wound up as a Tech Sgt. I'm glad you got that extra rank. If anybody deserved it, you did.

Over and out Lloyd

# LETTER NUMBER 11
OCTOBER 8, 1998

Dear Lloyd:

I got your pictures. It seems that the years have been pretty good to you. I think that is the result of being busy and not just sitting and letting yourself get old. I am still very active. I closed my business about six years ago and the next day got active in market research. I take jobs that suit me and generally work anywhere from ten hours to eighty hours a week. It keeps the rust off.

I have never been able to count the number of B-17s that were shot down but my guess is that probably no more than half of the crews that participated ever completed their tour I'm referring to those missions that we flew before "D" Day. After that they were mostly milk runs. They were missions with high numbers of planes taking part with proportionately few losses. After "D" Day there were escorts all the way to and from the target. You will remember that practically no missions were flown for a ninety day period ending in January 1944. Then when we started again, there were more B-17s, but still no escort to the target.

Let me go back to our days at Pyote, Texas. We were new to each other and just getting acquainted. One of our waist gunners, Jack Ward, who later left the crew to go to pilot training as an aviation cadet, always was complaining of feeling air sick. I had him down to the flight surgeon several times but without a lot of success. Well, one morning when we had landed after our morning flight, the crew took off like there was no tomorrow. Usually the crew would walk back to operations as a group, discussing the flight, what went right, what went wrong. Then the crew chief told me that some one had gotten sick in the waist of

171

the plane. I assured him that it would be cleaned up, and called the rapidly disappearing crew back.

I had inspected the plane before we took off and knew that it was clean. The dirty spot was back in the waist, and since none of the officers had been to the rear of the cockpit, I excused them I told the crew to sit down under the wing, out of the sun until we decided who got sick. I said we had nothing scheduled until the next morning, and if it took until then to decide who got sick then that's how long we were going to sit under the wing. The crew sat under the right wing and I sat under the left wing so they would have some privacy to discuss the problem. Poor Jack Ward kept saying, "I know you think it was me, but it wasn't." He was right, I really thought he was the guilty party. Then someone said that he would clean it up. I asked if he got sick. He said "No." then I said "Then you won't clean it up. Then the whole crew volunteered to clean it up. I asked if they all got sick. Of course the answer was no. I said "Then you all won't clean it up." About an hour had passed by this time and I thought I was going to lose the confrontation.

Suddenly one of the crew spoke up and admitted to being sick. I told him to go ahead and clean it up. He wanted to know if that was all. I told him yes that's all. Several other members of the crew asked if they could help. I told them that anyone who wanted to help, could help. I explained to them that all I wanted was the truth, and I wanted it right away. I told them that we would have a meeting at my barracks after lunch.

After lunch the crew met with me and we had a long talk. I explained that I was responsible for them and it was absolutely necessary that anytime there was a problem that I had to know about it first and I had to know the truth. If there was to be any coloring added to the story, I would supply it. I did not want to be blindsided. The crew member who had been sick said that if he had understood this he would have owned up immediately. He said he was afraid that he would be dropped from the crew.

After this understanding, on occasion I would be awakened at night with the whole crew there to report some difficulty they had. Most times I never heard about the incident but I was always prepared. I think the incident of the sickness in the plane helped mold the crew into a unit. Incidentally, I don't remember who got sick.

Several months later on our way overseas, the benefits of the sickness incident were shown vividly. We had picked up our brand new B-17 at Kearney Nebraska and our first stop was at Syracuse, N.Y. We were instructed to place a 24 hour guard on the plane. I arranged a schedule and as I remember Sam Bell had the shift ending at midnight. Wes Creech was to relieve him. The plane was parked in a disbursal area and after looking for the plane for an hour, he could not find it in the dark. He went to operations and explained his problem requesting that they have some one drive him to find the plane. They refused. Bell waited for his relief until 2:30 A.M. before leaving the plane. The next morning when I got back to the base the crew met me and told me all the details. Almost immediately I got word to report to operations. When I arrived they got on my back about the plane not being guarded and what a serious matter it was. They indicated this would be brought to the attention of the C.O. However I was in possession of all the facts and after laying them out to the operations officer, I told him I thought we should see the C.O. at once. Now we had a completely different situation and he thought there was no need to see the C.O., that it was only a misunderstanding. I agreed and left while I was ahead.

Only part of this probably was known to you, but the complete cooperation and confidence between crew members dated back to our meeting in Pyote regarding the sickness incident, many months before.

Well I'm about typed out for now, let me know if you remember the sickness incident and the meeting.

Over and out, Reddo

*James J. "Reddo" Redmond, Jr.*

# LETTER NUMBER 12
OCTOBER 31, 1998

Dear Reddo:

Good to hear from you again, I have to confess that most of what you talked about, the mess in the plane. I can't remember. I would like to tell you again that I had the hardest time adjusting to flying. I know you were aware of it at the time. I would take a can with me on all of our flights because I knew what was going to happen, but I never threw up on the floor. I was never in the waist section after we left the ground. I don't know who the guilty party was, but while we are on the subject (since I had a serious problem adjusting to flying because of air sickness). You and I had a serious talk about it. You told me that you didn't think I was going to make it. I asked you to let me try it for a couple more weeks and if I couldn't make it, I'd do what you wanted me to do. I want you to know that shortly after that I threw away my can, I stopped getting air sick. Can you remember talking to me about this?

There had to be many conversations that took place but most of them I can't remember. Even some of the missions I can't remember the details. All the hard ones I can. Reddo, that was fifty four years ago. You and I have been lucky. Life has been good to us. I wish there was some way of knowing if the rest of the crew has been as fortunate.

Do you recall the briefing we had on one of our missions to Schweinfurt? That it had to be wiped off the map. That it was a ball bearing plant and vital to the German war effort and it had to be wiped out. I think we took care of this.

We made many rough and tough missions and somehow survived.  You are right when you said that less than half the crews made it through their tour of duty.  Every time I remember what we accomplished while flying as a team in the Eighth Air Force gives me a good proud feeling on the inside.  I still consider it my greatest accomplishment in my life.  We were put to the test and all came through with flying colors.

I do my writing at night while everything is quiet and still.  My wife goes to bed about ten o'clock and I put the T V on mute and I can concentrate much better.  She fell and got a fracture of the spine.  It's taking her a while to get over it.

Reddo, I never did ask you how many kids you and your wife had.  I know you have some.  Once before when we were communicating, I heard a bunch of kids in the background and you had to ask them to be quiet so we could talk.  I told you about my first wife.  We married just before we went overseas and it didn't work out.  I waited too long to remarry, and the woman I married already had her family and It was too late for us.  I still claim them as my own, so we have three daughters, seven grand children, and two great grand children.  Our anniversary is coming up November 5. We'll be married thirty four years.

All for now,

Radio to Pilot, over and out.

*James J. "Reddo" Redmond, Jr.*

# LETTER NUMBER 13
November 8, 1998

Dear Lloyd:

Now that you mention it, I do remember that you had a problem with air sickness. I do remember our discussions about it. I remember how happy and relieved I was when you told me you had overcome your problem. I remembered Jack Ward more because he complained about it all the time. Actually I was not too upset when Ward was accepted for pilot training. I didn't think he fit together with the crew as well as the others. I might have been wrong and I worked with him and the flight surgeon to give him a fair chance but it didn't make any difference since he went to the cadet program.

With you it worked out easier. You just recovered on your own and that was that. When we got Pop Beyer, he fit in and our crew was complete.

I wonder if you remember the 48 hour pass we all took to go to Leeds? We had heard such wild tales about the Robin Hood that they were too wild to believe. We had to go see for ourselves. We had the pass arranged, and we were ready to go, when we were put on a loading for the same day. Of course the mission took precedence over any pass, so we prepared for the mission. As I recall, wake up was for 1:30 Am with take off set for 6:00 AM. We were in the plane ready for take off when a series of delays occurred. Take off was delayed a half hour at a time until 11:00 AM when the mission was scrubbed. Now our leave was in effect again. The last bus left for Peterborough at 11:45 AM and lunch was not served "till noon. We all skipped lunch and caught the bus. We arrived in Peterborough after all the lunch rooms had closed: however the bar in the railroad station was open and serving. We drank English beer until the train left for Leeds just before the restaurants opened for dinner. When the train arrived in Leeds, the restaurants had closed. I'm not going into all that happened at the Robin Hood, it is enough to say that the next day I felt as bad as I have ever felt. I did not even see you guys the next morning. I just left wherever I had spent the night and caught the train back to the base. When I got there I was beginning to feel a little more human, but the whole base was in a state of depression. They had flown the exact same mission we had been briefed for the previous day. About half of the group formation had been shot down. What impressed me most of all was that the crew which flew in our position had been shot down.

I did not know the crew. It was their first mission. We were sure lucky that we were off getting plastered instead of being on that mission. There was some talk about whether the Germans knew all about the mission and were ready for them, Do you remember this? I do not remember if the whole crew went or not. I think so because we usually did things as a unit. I do remember arriving at the Robin Hood after you guys had obtained a large round table. I had been trying to find a hotel room (unsuccessfully). There were no extra chairs and I had an argument with an RAF pilot about whose chair he was sitting on. We decided that since he was already there when I arrived, that it must be his.

About that time a young lady suggested that it was too crowded in here and that we should go to another place that she recommended. We did.

We were certainly lucky to go on leave instead of on that mission. I guess the good Lord was watching over us even if He took us into a den of iniquity to keep us safe. If we did anything wrong, it would be His fault.

Yes, I have three children. Two girls and one boy. The girls have been married and are divorced. My son is unmarried and is

177

living with me.  He is a used car dealer.  I have two grandchildren and three great grandchildren.

I don't think that you heard any kids when we were on the phone because they all live in Buffalo.  What you heard was Barney, the parrot.  He sometimes carries on so that it sounds like people.

Yes I remember the briefing on Schweinfurt.  Actually we went to Schweinfurt several times.  This was such a fearful mission because of earlier missions and because it was so heavily defended.  We did plaster it pretty good, but it was a long way from the most scary mission we were on.

The missions had to be scary when you recognize that over 6,500 heavy American bombers of the Eighth Air Force were shot down in combat over Europe.  That does not include damaged planes of which there were many.  As a matter of fact, we rarely came back without damage of some sort.  We were most lucky that the hits we sustained were not critical.  If they were, we would not be here to correspond.  Let me know what you remember about Leeds.  I'll talk about our flak leave in Southport next time.

Pilot to radio over and out.

# LETTER NUMBER 14
## NOVEMBER 25, 1998

Dear Reddo:

Yes, I do remember almost all about the Leeds week end pass...As I remember almost all the crew went except Beyers and Wagner. I really got tickled the way you put it together. I mean you remembered it right. We sure missed about three meals just so we could get to Leeds. We were in bad shape for any kind of drinking. You made me feel sorry for you just by reading your letter. I could feel just about as bad as you must have felt coming back to the base at Polebrook and finding out what had happened while we were gone on leave. You brought back my memory about this. This was in 1944. Correct me if I'm wrong. It's been a long time ago. But what I want here is if you remember how easy it was to pick up a woman. Those women in England had their eyes on an American service man. The men didn't like us but the women did. On this occasion we couldn't shake one woman and she came all the way back to Peterborough with us. She latched on to me and I finally talked another soldier into taking her off my hands. I had to get back to the base. This was quite an experience.

Reddo, I've thought about our missions a jillion times, and as I've expressed in my past letters, as I look back, these were the proudest moments of my life. I know looking back we wrote a page in history that will never be forgotten. How we got through it was by the grace of God. I saw so many bullet holes and flak holes throughout the whole plane. I wish I had pictures of it on both sides.

Reddo, about Leeds. There was a group of ladies there who called themselves The Seven Virgins. I don't think you ever got in on this one. I want to tell you about my experiences in Southport when we correspond next.

I can type and I have a good electric typewriter, but I'm not a good typist, and besides my wife goes to bed about 10:00 PM, and the typewriter would wake her up. I enjoy corresponding with you. You are a link to the past that I still like to remember. I hope it will continue.

I flew five or six missions after you finished because I had to be hospitalized with conjunctivitis caused by a loose fitting oxygen mask. I was in the hospital two weeks. Both eyes had to be lanced. It's dangerous flying high altitude in many ways. But it's over now and all that's left is the memories and I enjoy them.

I don't remember whether I told you that I re-enlisted after I got back to the States or not. I remember telling you about my first marriage and how bad it turned out to be. I was so torn up and unsettled that I thought the best place to be was the place I was familiar with, so I re-enlisted for three more years in Alaska and the Elution Islands.

Do you remember the double shots of whisky they gave us just before we entered the briefing room or rather the de-briefing room (to loosen us up), and boy it made me half drunk.

Reddo, I know the crew of Reddo's Raiders has made its record in the downfall of Hitler and his gang and their dream of ruling the world. Not one of them has survived as far as I know. I know that you and I survived and I hope that more of our crew is still living today.

We are planning on a Thanksgiving Dinner at home. I think this is the correct way of having a Thanksgiving dinner. I hope Thanksgiving will be a joyous occasion for you and your family.

Till next time.

Radio to pilot, over and out.

# LETTER NUMBER 15
## DECEMBER 13, 1998

Dear Lloyd:

Thinking back to the Leeds Trip, I did miss the Seven Virgins in Leeds. As I remember, I was too drunk and too involved with my own virgin to accompany the rest of you. Was it as rowdy as the Robin Hood?

Let me tell you a little about my experience. My lady at the Robin Hood suggested that we go some place else since there were no chairs available for us. Since I was incapable of rational thought, I agreed. I don't know the name of the place we went but it was pretty rowdy. It was not as crowded as the Robin Hood. Since I had not been able to find anyplace to stay for the night, she suggested a rooming house or a boarding house. I agreed and as we waited in the taxi office, she called the landlady and told her what we had in mind. I remember her telling the landlady that I was a Yank. Then, Oh yes Mum, he's a lovely Yank. I guess the landlady accepted us and we got a cab to the house. We had a room on the fourth floor, and the bathroom was on the third floor. During the night I got sick (surprised). To get to the bathroom I had to go down a long hall, down the stairs, down another hall. All of this bare ass naked. I guess I made a real sight. However I didn't meet another soul during my trip. In my condition, I didn't give a shit.

Came morning, I had the granddaddy of hangovers. All I wanted to do was get out of there, get some fresh air and go back to the base. I had all the carousing I could handle for a while. I didn't know where to look for the crew. After I got dressed. I hiked down all four flights of stairs and started out the front door. Now appeared the land lady who said "You haven't had your breakfast yet". I told her I didn't want any breakfast. Believe me I couldn't have eaten anything if my life depended on it. She said" you must come in and have some tea beans and toast". I finally convinced her that I would not eat. (I guess it was a boarding house where meals are provided for the guests. Then she said" But you haven't washed up". I told her I had washed up stairs. She then said" But you couldn't have, for I didn't draw water for you"(I guess the bathroom did not have a wash basin. I don't remember).It hurt my head so much to argue that I agreed to come back and wash. While I waited in the parlor my lady came down from upstairs to visit with me. No matter how bad I felt, we had to visit. This was the first time I really got a look at her. While she was really attractive, she was not the beauty that was with me the night before. She was so tiny that her feet didn't touch the floor when she sat on a chair. The landlady brought in a basin and a pitcher of warm water. In the parlor I washed to everyone's satisfaction, put on my clothes and said good by.

When I walked out the front door and down the steps, I realized that I did not have the foggiest idea where I was. Since I felt so bad, I decided to walk thinking the fresh air would help. I started toward where I thought the center of town might be. I was right. I walked for about two and a half hours and luckily I found the railroad station. I wanted to find the crew, but I didn't have any idea of where to look. So, having no way to find the crew, I decided to go back to the base. I still had another day of leave, but I was in not in any condition to enjoy it. I think I told you in my last letter what happened in the mission they flew while we were gone. Incidentally, the train was so crowded that I had to stand up almost all the way back to Peterborough.

About the rest of the crew, Marty Strom is deceased, also Shorty Palmer. I have contacted Tony Wagner and Sam Bell. If you want to contact them, here are their addresses:

Tony Wagner <DELETED>
Sam Bell <DELETED>

The telephone number I had for Vinson has been disconnected. I have numbers for Creech and Cavanaugh but have not gotten any answers.

I spelled Beyer's name wrong when I requested it and I do not have any reply on a re-request. I will be surprised if Beyer is still alive. He would be way up in his eighties. I hope I can find him, so I'll keep on trying.

You keep expecting that history will remember what we did. I am not so optimistic. I had a look in a high school history book and world war two was covered in two pages. No mention at all of the Eighth Air Force or the Air war in Europe. Just be proud of what you did and the 65,000 casualties of the Eighth Air Force and the 6,533 heavy American bombers shot down. Our contribution to victory.

Incidentally I am enclosing a summary of the losses of planes by the 351st Bomb Group. I think you will find it eye opening.

Let me hear from you. I would like to know about the Seven Virgins. I missed that entirely. I wondered where you found seven virgins in Leeds.

Pilot to radio, over and out.

*James J. "Reddo" Redmond, Jr.*

# LETTER NUMBER 16
JANUARY 3, 1999

Dear Reddo:

I was amazed that you came up with the bundle of information about the Eighth Air Force missions. I wonder if you have been digging into the public information of Eighth Air Force Archives in Washington DC. The statistics are so amazing, or should I say staggering. I knew our losses were great, but I never thought they were as much as you wrote me. I knew already we were lucky to come through it with hardly a scratch "so to speak". You and I were the only members of the crew that got any injuries at all, and My Princess was literally shot full of holes, mostly by flak, although we got our share of German fighters. I know Marty Strom got credit for at least one fighter. I don't know whether any of the rest of the crew got any credit or not for shooting a German plane down. Maybe you can fill me in on this.

Have you been in touch with Frank Urbanek, membership Chairman? I think I sent you his letter. He wrote to me.

I was sorry to hear about the passing of Marty Strom and Vern Palmer. I have thought this would be the way many times. I hope there is no more of the crew that has passed on.

There is still a sad note to the saga of the crew. I talked to Sam Bell three or four days ago and he had a stroke on his right side that has left him 30% paralyzed. He can't write very good. It takes him a lot longer to write than it would if he was normal. I talked with him for about an hour. We had a very enjoyable visit. His mind is clear and he remembers things as good as he ever could. I think it happened in June 1994, and the sad part is, his wife has to take dialysis. It's a kidney problem plus she has high

184

blood pressure. I gave him your telephone number so don't be surprised if he calls you.

About the Seven Virgins. It wasn't a club, but a big two story house where seven nice looking women lived. They were working women. They weren't whores. They were like we were. They wanted a good time and they shared their good times with us when we were there. I wish you could have experienced it. You would have never forgotten it. Sam Bell mentioned it when I talked with him, and He remembered some things I had forgotten. They always cooked our breakfast the next morning. It must have been a thing with those English women. They thought they needed to cook your breakfast before you left. But we always left the Seven Virgins plenty of money. They enjoyed it as much as we did. It was quite an experience I'll never forget. They had a bed in the living room and me and my date were sitting in different chairs talking, and along came palmer and his girl friend.

They decided to put on a show. They both got in bed and did they ever put on a show. You know what I mean,

I'm going to get in touch with Tony Wagner and see how he's doing,

Thank you for all the information and stats. You are still a go getter.

Radio to pilot over and out.

*James J. "Reddo" Redmond, Jr.*

# LETTER NUMBER 17
## JANUARY 7, 1999

Dear Lloyd:

I know that you will be surprised to receive a reply so soon; actually, I don't have any work this week, so I thought I would write back at once.

I know that the summary of losses of the 351st was an eye opener for you. It certainly was for me. I put it together from several sources, primarily from the history of the 351st written by Peter Harris and Ken Harbour. They were two Englishmen who selected the 351st to research and publish. It is about one hundred pages plus a section of pictures, not numbered. The title is "The 351st Bomb Group in World War Two." If you are interested you might be able to get a copy from the 351st Bomb Group Association. I don't remember the price or know whether any are available.

The photo of "My Princess" was supposed to be on the dust cover, but publication was so rushed that the dust cover was never made. The picture of "My Princess" that I sent you was to be the picture used.

As I remember, Strom got credit for a confirmed kill, and Creech, Bell and Palmer shared in two other confirmed. I think Wagner also got in on this. I do remember clearly that the fighter that was blown up directly in front while on a head on attack blew into so many pieces that it was almost as dangerous flying through the debris as allowing them to shoot at us. We did take some damage from some of the smaller pieces hitting our plane, but nothing critical. This was the explosion that blew the German's right wing man into Strom's line of fire where he shot off the tail.

This all happened on the raid on Ludwigshaven on May 27, 1944. The one where you didn't know that all hell was breaking loose, since most of the action was up front and out of your line of vision.

A letter to Frank Cavanaugh was returned marked "deceased", and a letter to Jack Vinson was returned marked "Forwarding address expired". I have written the Chamber of Commerce in Union S.C. asking if they could help in locating him.

Referring to the losses of the 351st, you may remember the 100th Bomb Group, better known as "The Bloody Hundredth". On one of their missions they sent thirteen planes out, one returned. I don't remember what raid this was on, I just remember the talk about their losses. They were a real hard luck group. Actually they must have flown lousy formation, because that's what attracts fighters. I had a very close buddy in the 100th. He was a co-pilot. He received the Silver Star for a mission where his pilot had his head blown off by a cannon shell in the cockpit. My friend was not wounded, and flew the plane back to England after pulling it out of a steep spiral.

Do you remember anything about our "Flak Leave" in Southport? You remember they gave us an all expense ten day vacation at a resort about half way through our tour. This was supposed to refresh us so we could complete our missions. Do you remember the ladies we picked up in that hotel bar? They had an older woman who was keeping an eye on them. Every one had been paired off, and as I remember, I had the prettiest one of the group. At first I thought the old lady was a madam taking her girls out for some fun. This was not the case, and as nearly as I could figure it out, some of the girls were domestics and the old lady was taking them out. I don't think she counted on meeting up with any Yankee Air men. I remember we wound up at a dance where we learned to do the "Hokey Pokey". I had a number of dates with my lady. I believe that both she and her mother were in service at a very plush residence where I called for her.

*James J. "Reddo" Redmond, Jr.*

I don't remember whether or not you were foolish enough to go for a swim at Southport. I was. It was the coldest water I have ever been in. Well that's all for now.

Pilot to radio, over and out.

# LETTER NUMBER 18
JANUARY 25, 1999

Dear Reddo:

I just finished reading your letter for about the fourth or fifth time. I always read them over and over again to make sure I absorb all of it. All of your letters are so interesting. I'm really glad you have dug up so much information on the 351st and the statistics of our losses. I was floored at first, and am still amazed at the staggering losses we suffered from flak and air to air combat. Thank you for remembering who in the crew got credit for kills. I'm surprised that the ball turret, Bell, didn't receive at least one kill. He had such a good view of everything from below. I told you about talking to Bell on the telephone for about an hour and found out about him having a stroke that left him 30% paralyzed on the right side. I haven't talked to Wagner but I'm going to. Thank you for giving me their "phone numbers and addresses.

It saddens me to hear about the passing of three of the crew members so far and it could be more. You have done a remarkable job already, and I congratulate you. You are still on the ball.

I remember Southport and the dates we had with the madam and her girls. They were a lot of fun. I'll have to agree with you about you having the best looking one. You really had a cutie, but I had a good looking one too. In fact as I remember they were all good looking. I don't remember about the cold water because I didn't go swimming. I could go into another date but it would take too long to explain it.

About The Seven Virgins in Leeds. It wasn't a night club, but was a big two story building where seven women lived. You talk about a ball when all of us got together. It was unbelievable. Palmer and his girl put a show on one night in the living room right before me and my girls eyes. If I live to be a hundred, I'll never forget it. I think you know what I mean. We always called each other by our last names, and I still feel comfortable doing that. Creech and I were the only married men on the crew (as I remember). I married on a six day delay en route from Pyote Texas to Alexandria, La. The worst mistake I ever made in my life. Of course I'm happily married now, but those war time marriages just don't pan out. Didn't you say you were in a marketing business?

Reddo, I'm going to make my assessment to you of what I think. We both went through very dangerous and difficult times and we are both fortunate to get through safely. I didn't think so much about it then because I was young and I flew one mission at a time. Now when I look back on it, I realize that we had less than a 50/50 chance of ever making it back in one piece. I realize how we all put ourselves in harms way. I always thought of you as being the greatest pilot that ever sat in a cock pit. I've said it before and I'll say it again, if anybody could bring us home safely, you could.

Even though I think of myself as being in good shape health wise, my wife is not. She has to get around in a quad cone or a walker. She has a compound fracture of the spine from a fall. I'm not complaining, that's not my nature. I'm thankful that I'm still able to wait on her.

Reddo, I still think we had our day in the sun and when the last page is written the 351st will go down in history as one of the greatest groups of fighting men that was ever assembled. This includes the whole Eighth Air Force.

I hope you keep researching the rest of the crew. I would like to know if they are OK. I shut everything down when I'm writing you. I want it to be quiet. I'm looking for your letter.

Radio to pilot over and out.

190

# LETTER NUMBER 19
JANUARY 30, 1999

Dear Lloyd:

Just had some bad news. Vinson died on December 8, 1998. If I had started sooner we might have had an opportunity to talk to him. Actually, probably not. He might not have been able to respond. I don't have any idea how he died or what illness he had. I got my information from an inquiry to the Chamber of Commerce in Union, South Carolina, the ranks get thinner.

You may remember Bud Ritzema, pilot of a crew all through training with us. He was a member of the 351st, but in a different squadron. He was shot down on February 22, 1944 during a raid during "Big Week." I was able to locate him. He is not doing too badly, but not in the same shape as you and I.

As I remember Sam Bell did get credit for a part kill with the others on that Ludwigshaven raid. If I left his name out when I wrote before, it was by accident. I always respected him for riding in the ball turret. I rode in it a number of times only to familiarize myself with the position. Until you got used to it was scary hanging out below the plane. I would not have liked to serve in that position for a whole mission.

As you probably know the 351st is having their reunion in Savannah, Georgia next June. I think it is the first week. I am planning on attending. Regardless of how well I am doing age has a funny way of screwing things up, and I might not be able to go at another time. Savannah is not very far from Florida.

I am sorry to hear that your wife is in such a difficult condition. What are her prospects for a full recovery?

Oh! Before I forget, Ritzema's co-pilot, Paul Straw, rose to the rank of Major General. He is probably retired by now. That's ridiculous, of course he's retired, he would be almost eighty years old.

As you probably know the 351st is having their reunion in Savannah, Georgia next June. Savannah is not really that far from Oklahoma. Maybe if you planned a little bit you could make it. Maybe your wife will recover enough to accompany you. It might be the last time we will be able to see whatever guys are left. Think about that.

Do you remember when we were in Goose Bay Labrador? We were on our way overseas and had flown up from Presque Isle Maine. We had messed around all day not resting or anything. About dinner time we were notified that we were to take off that night to fly the Atlantic to England. I did not say anything to the crew or anyone else, but I had decided I was not going to fly the Atlantic in the winter time without a good nights sleep. So without saying anything we went about getting ready to go. Of course we had to get gassed up. There were gas trucks all over the ramp stopping whenever a plane signaled that they needed to get gassed up. I ignored them and waited until all the trucks had gone back to the motor pool. We had to take off before midnight or there would not be enough darkness for celestial navigation. When all the gas trucks had gone and it was almost midnight, I called the tower and complained that we needed to be gasses up. I said that the trucks had ignored my signals that we needed gas, and now I didn't see any trucks at all. The tower was really pissed off, but they got a truck to us. We got gassed up and I messed around for a while, then I called the tower for taxi instructions. I guess they had forgotten about us, and were all pissed off all over again. I was very calm and asked again for taxi instructions. They blew their top and said it was too late to go. I knew this, or I thought I did, because if they said go, I wouldn't have had any alternative except to go. They said to put the wing covers on and go back to the BOQ. The wind was blowing at twenty to thirty miles an hour, and the temperature was about thirty degrees below zero. I told the officers to go and the crew and I would put the wing covers on. This was a real chore, just when you thought you had one on, the wind would turn it into a sail. We finally got the plane put up but it took until three AM. Our delay in leaving kept us at Goose Bay for another ten days before the weather cleared.

Let me know if you remember the episode about their trying to get us out the day we arrived. You might not have been aware of what was going on with my delays, but I'll bet you remember putting those wing covers on.

Well that's about all for now, but think about the reunion, maybe we can get together there.

Pilot to radio, over and out.

James J. "Reddo" Redmond, Jr.

# LETTER NUMBER 20
FEBRUARY 14, 1999

Dear Reddo:

Was nice as always to hear from you, but was saddened about the news of Vinson's passing on. Thank you for your diligent efforts in bringing this to pass. It has been since late in 1944 that I had seen or heard from Vinson, but because of our closeness as a crew, knowing he's gone adds to the hurt and emptiness. I feel for him and the rest of the crew that we know has gone on. What Hitler and his henchmen could not do to us, Father Time has done to our crew. Four have fallen and one disabled because of a stroke. Three more to be accounted for. I wrote to Wagner about three weeks ago and haven't heard anything yet. I'm going to call and see if I can get a response.

I seem to remember about the wing covers but not in any detail. I don't think you ever told us about gassing up the plane. I remember the first time we tried to cross the Atlantic we had to abort because the wings were icing up so much the de-icing liquid couldn't handle it. Do you remember this? It has been over fifty four years since this happened.

Did Sam Bell ever call you? I gave him your telephone number. He told me he would call you.

Reddo, I am sorry to say this but I can't possibly go to the Eighth Air Force Reunion because of my wife's condition. She is still on a walker and she can't stay on her feet over five minutes at a time. I have to do all the cooking or take her out to eat. The doctor says it will take a long time for the compression of the spine to heal. I would like so very much to see you and hash over old times. I have yet to get a decent picture of you and your wife or any other pictures you wish to send me. I'm still working on a wide angle picture of me and my band in action to send you. So far I haven't found any one with that kind of a camera. By the way we play this Thursday night. I wish you could be here.

I can't remember Ritzema but I can remember the commander in charge when we went through all of our three phases of training. He was Captain Berkowitz. He went overseas with us and then I lost track of him. I'm sure you remember him. These memories are fond to me. It was the bonding together of a never forgettable group of men that achieved a place in history that I am still so proud that I was allowed to participate in. It was then and still is my proudest moment. When I think back, it was the greatest thing I ever did in my life, and I didn't even give it a second thought. I just considered it my patriotic duty and Reddo, I don't know if you have considered this the same way I have. You probably have but we could have been killed on any given mission.

It wasn't only the perils of dying by enemy gunfire and aircraft, we had to face the dangers of frost bite, by your oxygen going out, or by your oxygen mask not fitting properly. (like what happened to me) I don't know if you remember it or not, but my oxygen mask was too loose (probably my fault for not checking it) and it poisoned my eye lids. I had to have my eye lids lanced, and spent two weeks in the hospital.

I didn't get the last Polebrook paper for some reason. I'll have to find out why. That's the reason I didn't know about the place where the reunion will be held. You were the first to tell me.

Writing to you is good experience for me because it gives me a good reflection on my past, which is good. You are up front on everything and keep me informed. Thank you for the good job you have done in digging up information on the crew.

Radio to pilot, over and out.

*James J. "Reddo" Redmond, Jr.*

# LETTER NUMBER 21
## FEBRUARY 17, 1999

Dear Lloyd:

Just got your letter and am replying right away because I have something to enclose.

We had a visit from a B-17G this week, and along with it there was a breakfast meeting of Air Force Vets. Most of them were Eighth Air Force Vets. I wore my A-2 jacket which is painted with "My Princess", missions, dates, etc. It was a hit. I had already given it to my son, but borrowed it back. I got up and made a few comments to the group and had my picture taken. I'm enclosing a copy of the news article and the picture.

I served as one of the volunteers who answered questions from the people who came to look at the B-17. As at result of this I have been asked to speak at a meeting of gun and war memorabilia collectors. I have decided to accept their invitation. I'll let you know how it turns out.

I'm really sorry you can't attend the 351st reunion. That way I could be sure that there would be at least one person that I knew. Incidentally both of the fellows whose picture was taken with me were members of the 351st but they joined the group long after we had left for the States.

Yes I do remember the incident of the wings icing up so that we couldn't take off from Goose Bay. As I remember the engines also started to freeze up so that we had to take the plane to a hanger to thaw out. My best recollection is that it took several days to thaw out. Then the weather socked in. We were in Goose Bay for about ten days. We were there so long that some of the permanent party began to consider us as permanent personnel. The tee totaler base commander even opened the bar in the officer's club. This bar was kept closed so long as there were transient crews on the base.

We had gotten friendly with some of the permanent personnel and had made arrangements to take a truck and visit a Hudson's Bay Trading Post about thirty miles from the air base. We had used our plane to check out the road to the post to make sure it was open. The road was really a path. We were going to the post the next morning when lo and behold the weather cleared and they booted our asses out the night before the trip.

I have not heard from Bell. I had called him when I gave you his number. We had a nice conversation but nothing from him since. Bell may have a complex about his condition, but I don't know why Wagner never responded. You may not know but Wagner was a little retiring. He did not participate in the rowdy action with the rest of us. For example he did not go to Leeds with us. This would not be his cup of tea.

I wish we could have located Creech. I remember just before we were to leave Alexandria. Louisiana for Kearney Nebraska, those who had wives had them come down to say good by. We were all together (the whole crew and the wives) in a lounge (I don't remember where), and I told Creech that he had a beautiful wife.(she really was gorgeous). He would respond, "Yes, but she doesn't have a brain in her head. I couldn't believe what I was hearing. I wonder what happened to them.

Now here is a surprise for you. You mentioned that you had anniversary recently. Congratulations. I am sending a small gift for you to celebrate with your wife. When you see the brand you will know why I had to get it for you. The meeting I spoke about earlier in this letter was called, "A Gathering of Eagles", pretty smooth, huh?

*James J. "Reddo" Redmond, Jr.*

Don't apologize for writing. Your penmanship is easy to read. The only reason I type is because this is the only way I can be sure you will be able to read my letters.

I think you might remember Ritzema if you saw him. He was over six feet tall and had a big mustache. He weighed about 220 lbs. The gift which is on its way is probably a throw back to the bottle of whiskey we had on Christmas in 1943.

O K Your turn.

Pilot to radio, over and out.

# LETTER NUMBER 22
## MARCH 15, 1999

Dear Reddo:

Once again I must report bad news. Tony Wagner passed away this year. I talked with his brother and he told me that he died in his sleep. He lived with Tony. His brother was sixty nine and Tony was seventy seven. His brother told me that he had heart trouble for the past several years. He went in to wake him up and he was already dead. Tony never married, he told me, but his family must have loved him very much. There were nine children. Three sisters and one brother left.

I received a nice letter from his niece that I'm making a copy of and a picture of Tony. I'm sending them on to you. Her version of his death differs a little from his brothers, but I tend to agree with his brother since he lived with him. I know it left another empty hole in my heart. Tony wasn't an outgoing person, like you said in your letter, but he was a solid individual. He wasn't the partying type at all. I never remember him having a real date. I know he was with us in Southport and I guess he went to the dance with the rest of us but I don't know whether he picked him a girl or not. Maybe you do. I know Tony was a solid crew member and was a good bombardier. I have thought of him so many times as I have thought about the passing of all the other crew members. As you said in one of your letters, "The ranks are growing thinner".

I loved the way you performed at the breakfast meting of Air Force Vets. If you made the same convincing speech you made to each of before we ever flew a mission, I'm sure it was a good one. The picture you sent me was good and I'm sure your next speech at the gun and war memorabilia collectors will be just as impressive. I was proud of you as being my pilot and I'm proud of you now.

If it hadn't been for your effort, I would never known about the passing of Strom, Vinson, and Palmer. I thank you for your efforts. Now we have two more not accounted for, Creech and Beyers.

You mentioned a gift for me. I think I know what you are talking about but I have not received it yet. I wonder if it could have been lost in the mail.

I keep all of your letters and thinking back on what you told me about our losses, it was over sixty percent of our bombers that were lost. Correct me if I'm wrong but with these figures we had less that a fifty percent chance of coming through alive. Thank the Lord that we're still alive and kicking.

I can't understand why Bell has never called you unless he could have had another stroke. I think I'll call him again and find out. I hope it's not like it was with Tony. When I asked if I could speak with Tony his brother told me that he had passed away. I'm beginning to think we are not living in the land of the living, but in the land of the dying. But Reddo, this is not my true belief because I'm a Christian and have been for a number of years, ever since I was twenty nine. I've heard you mention something about the Lord being on our side when I read your account of all the missions we flew and the way you remembered them. I'm sending a copy to Tony's niece. I thought they were very good.

I want to reflect back a little and see if you remember when we left Presque Isle, Maine heading for Goose Bay Labrador. You asked me to get in touch with the ground station and check on the weather. I kept trying but must have been goofing or sleeping, and you kept trying to get in touch with the control tower. You finally did and they told you they were socked in and there was no way a plane could land on their runways because it was socked in with zero visibility. We had no choice but to turn around and return to Presque Isle, I wondered if you remembered this.

Radio to Pilot, over and out.

## LETTER NUMBER 23
APRIL 3, 1999

Dear Lloyd:

Sorry you had to call to make sure I hadn't joined our comrades. Actually I have been tremendously busy and didn't have time to write. I called Tony's brother and had a nice conversation with him. Thanks for sending me the copy of his brother's letter and his nieces. I got a real charge out of his nieces comment that Tony never mentioned the event in Southport with the lady and the girls. I don't remember whether Tony went to the dance or not. I seem to remember that he just excused himself and went elsewhere. As I remember that affair, we were all sitting at a large table having a beer, when I excused myself to go to the loo. (remember that word) When I got back to the table you guys had a whole group of girls (very pretty as I recall) at the table. The one that I fancied was very excited to find out that I was the "Skipper". We went on from there to the dance. I think Tony left us to go off on his own. I could be wrong about this, maybe he did go to the dance with us. There was never anything different about Tony I always thought he was a little square and bashful.

About the gift, I checked with the post office and the best advice they could come up with was to suggest that you check with the post office that services you and tell them that a package sent from Dania Beach, Florida was never received, and ask them to check if it might be misplaced in their office. It actually has a small dollar value and I did not insure it, so if it is not there some one else has it. Let me know because if it is not recovered I want to replace it.

It surprised me that you remembered the flight from Presque Isle, Maine to Goose Bay Labrador. I thought I was the only one to remember that. Your recollection was right on target. We left Presque Isle in late morning in beautiful weather. It was only a couple of hours flight to Goose Bay, and when we got there was a big cloud right over the air field. We then flew back to Presque Isle. This reminded me of a character in the comic "Lil Abner" named Joe Bffzsk. Joe always walked around with a big black cloud over his head. The worst was always about to happen to him. Do you remember this cartoon? I guess the problem of raising them on the radio was due to that storm cloud. Oh well we were having such a good time trying to get overseas that nothing fazed us. Do you remember that we were on per diem and the longer our trip took, the more money we got? I remember this clearly. We got $186.00 per diem. It took some rationalism on my part, but every enlisted man got the same as the officers. I remember in several stations where we overnighted, the enlisted men were charged twenty five cents for lodging. I maintained that anytime an enlisted man was charged a penny for sleeping he was not furnished adequate quarters. It cost the government $1,860.00 to get us overseas to win the war. Do you remember that payment. That was a considerable sum in those days. I would guess that it amounted to about two months pay for you buck sergeants.

We had some memorable experiences during our trip overseas. It took almost a month for us to get over. If you remember any of them, mention them, and I'll see if I can elaborate on them. Don't wait as long to write as I did.

Pilot to radio, over and out.

# LETTER NUMBER 24
APRIL 27, 1999

Dear Reddo;

Glad to receive your letter although I was worried somewhat. Time has a way of passing without us knowing it. I'm about as guilty as anyone to let time slip by.

I've been catching up on things that I've been neglecting too long such as painting. When I paint I get it all over me, but I finally get it done.

My wife seems to be getting better but not well enough for me to go to the reunion. Reddo, I've got a confession to make that you might find hard to believe. I'm afraid to fly anymore. It's something I can hardly explain. You know how hard it was for me to adjust to flying and after I came back to the States I was assigned as an instructor to fly with radio operators who didn't have combat experience on one flight my pilot and another pilot flying right wing decided they were good enough to overlap their wings. I knew that the slightest drift in wind direction or pressure could cause both planes to come crashing down. That's when I knew I had enough. I had flown thirty five combat missions (actually thirty three) and I didn't intend to get killed by a couple of bad pilots that didn't know what it was to fly combat. I reported the incident to the commanding officer and both pilots were grounded for a while. I don't know if it was the right thing to do but I felt that both pilots put both air crews of the aircraft in jeopardy.

Reddo, don't worry about the gift. It is good enough to know you sent it to me. I know what it was,

I finally got the post and saw your letter in there telling about our mission to Ludwigshaven. Before I got to where you signed off

*James J. "Reddo" Redmond, Jr.*

I knew it was you. I knew it was you because of the way you express yourself. It was about the same way you explained it to me. I couldn't see as you could because the radio operator has limited view.

The article below your article written by James H. Harris doesn't say what his position was, but says he was part of a crew flying in "MY Princes" on June 21, 1944 (target Berlin). This is not possible. We (Reddo's Raiders) were flying in "My Princess" on "D" Day June 6, 1944.That's only seventeen days apart. There's got to be a mistake here. You flew your last mission on June 20, 1944 to Hamburg. This was the last time I flew with you. Could it be that another crew was assigned the next day and flew "My Princess" on her forty sixth? I need more information if you can help me on this.

I remember all about the trip from Presque Isle to Goose Bay. As I remember we had to guard the plane all the way to Polebrook. Syracuse was great but after we left there the fun was behind us until we got to England.

The per diem was great but I didn't have time to spend it so I guess I must have sent it home to my wife and she spent it.

Reddo, you talk about great times. I've had a great time all my life. That's what life is all about to me. What gives me the greatest satisfaction is knowing I was part of a team that brought peace to the planet and to this day others are doing the same thing. Freedom is worth fighting and dying for, or as a poet once wrote, "The only thing it takes for evil to survive is for good men to say nothing".

Keep writing, I enjoy your letters very much. Help me out on this "My Princess" problem. I was not there when she was born, but I was there when she died. I put her in mothballs.

Radio to pilot, over and out.

# LETTER NUMBER 25
MAY 1, 1999

Dear Lloyd:

I decided to answer your letter right away because you were concerned about the letter published in the Polebrook Post regarding "My Princess".

Harris' comments were accurate. As you said we flew "My Princess" on June 6, 1944. There is no question about that. You are also correct that my last mission was on June 20, 1944. Since I finished my tour on June 20th, "My Princess" was assigned to another crew on the 21st. The pilots name was Lt. Hibbard. His whole crew bailed out over Germany except for the pilot, the co-pilot and the navigator. They could not make it back to Polebrook and landed at Beccles. Apparently the ship was damaged so badly that it was not fit for a return to combat, but was repaired and returned to the States.

Another ship of the 509th squadron, #42-97144 developed mechanical problems and crash landed in Sweden. The pilots name was Lt. Walters. I don't know if this plane had a name or not. Since he crash landed, it seems as though he had battle damage as well as mechanical trouble.

I don't see any conflict with the new crew flying "My Princess" after we were finished. Only be thankful that we were not flying her when she was crippled.

Now about the gift. Since you know what it is, please tell me. If you are correct, I'll drop it. If you are wrong I'll replace it.

*James J. "Reddo" Redmond, Jr.*

You were absolutely correct in reporting the performance of those two pilots. There is no place for formation flying when you have not been trained for it. Before we got into combat with close formation, I had many hours of training and practice in the states, in addition to which we practiced between missions.

I am glad your wife is improving. I hope she makes a full recovery. Maybe now that she is showing improvement, the healing process will speed up.

You had mentioned once before that she visited a relative and had a pleasant week. If she is improved, perhaps she would enjoy another visit, and that would leave you free to attend the reunion. It is only for five days. It would be good to see you again and this is probably the last opportunity. I do not anticipate going to another one. The next one will be a long distance from here. Let me know.

Radio from pilot, over and out.

# LETTER NUMBER 26
JUNE 8, 1999

Dear Lloyd:

Just got back from the reunion. It was great. I got there on June 1st and left on June 6th. I think every one forgot this was "D" day in Normandy. I know I didn't think of it until I had already checked out of the hotel.

As far as meeting people I remembered, there were not very many of them. I think this is because most of the crews who flew before "D" Day did not survive the war. Most of the men I became friendly with flew in late 1944 and early 1945. A lot of them didn't even get to England until 1945. However you can't fault them, It wasn't their choice. I did meet several men who were flying before "D" Day and a few who were flying in 1943, when it was really rough. Most of these were P.O.W.s who had eight or ten missions before they got knocked off. However as rough as some of their missions were, they had their share of milk runs just over the coast into France, when they had escort from the RAF in their Spitfires.

Did you have correspondence with Leonard Walline? It seems to me that you did. I had correspondence with him, and met him at the reunion. We talked some. He was shot down on his second mission which was Ludwigshaven on May 27, 1944. That was the rough one. He seemed to be in good health, but I suspect he had a stroke of some kind along the way, because it was sometimes to understand his speech.

I did meet Clay Pinner. He is an official of the Association. We remembered each other. He was a bombardier and was assistant group bombardier for a while. I also met Frank Hatten, a pilot who was being broken in for group lead` when he was shot down.

Captain Clay was the pilot breaking him in when they got shot down on the raid to Berlin. This is the raid when I took over the group lead after Hatten and Clay were shot down and led the group through the bomb run and over the target.

The next reunion will be in San Diego, California. They considered St. Louis, but there was too much pressure for California. I doubt that I will be able to afford the trip, but who knows? Never say never.

The Eighth Air Force Museum is fabulous. The only thing it lacks is a full size B-17. There is a sixteen minute film showing a complete mission, wake up, breakfast, briefing, get ready, and a mission. It alone was worth the trip. If you ever get the chance to go there, do it.

The other pilot in our crew picture was or is Don Mc Lott. You remember he joined our crew just before we left for overseas, and got his own crew right after we joined the 351st. That was when we got Cavanaugh as co-pilot. Cavanaugh was original cadre with the group having gone overseas with them on the Queen Mary. I don't remember why he was without a crew. Probably his crew got shot down while he was not with them.

Sorry Lloyd, you are wrong about the surprise. A good guess, but no cigar. As soon as I have a chance to visit the store again I will send you another. This time I will insure it so you will get it. I am glad that Christmas bottle of liquor made such an impression. I can hardly remember it.

You remarked about my statistics regarding the 351st and the air war. Some of them I got from the History Channel on T.V. Just recently it was announced that the Eighth Air Force had more killed in action than the U.S. Navy and the Marines combined. This is killed in action, it does not include wounded.

I have written to James Harris who said he expected to attend the reunion. If he attended or not I don't know but I did not see him. There were over 350 in attendance.

I haven't heard from Bell since I last called him. I don't think he can write as a result of that stroke and he may be financially strapped so he can't afford to use the telephone. He was super friendly in conversation. He may be embarrassed because of his handicap. What do you think?

We are having a hell of a rain storm. It started about four AM and by eleven AM we had five inches of rain. It has been raining continuously since, so we must have about ten inches by now. The streets are flooded so I could not go to work today. We are located on high ground so we are not in any danger.

Well that's all for now. Over and out.

Reddo

James J. "Reddo" Redmond, Jr.

# LETTER NUMBER 27
JUNE 27, 1999

Dear Reddo:

It was good to hear that the reunion turned out real good for you. It's hard to realize that it has been fifty years plus five since "D" Day. No I don't remember Leonard Walline. If I ever did, I have forgotten. It's nice to rehash old experiences with someone who has gone through the same things that you have.

I called Bell four or five days ago and he seemed to be feeling real good. I must have talked to him for an hour or more. He told me a lot of things I didn't know. I didn't know that he and Creech were stationed at Amarillo Air Base when they came back from overseas. He filled me in on all kinds of trouble Creech and his wife had while stationed at Amarillo. They finally separated and then divorced. I was sorry to hear about it because the same thing happened to me with my first marriage.

I talked to Bell about this mission to Manheim, on the Rhine River, about fifteen miles south of Aachen, Germany. He couldn't remember it either. I know the whole crew made the mission. I can remember this part clearly and there was no mission any rougher that this one. I had my doubts that we were ever going to see the English coast again. We (our squadron) had a maximum effort of thirteen planes and six were shot down. On most of the missions I didn't have a good vantage point, but on this one I did. Everything happened above me and behind me. I had a good view. I need to go to the library to locate Manheim. This has been a mystery ever since we first discussed it.

This is something else you may remember. Bell and I talked this over. He could remember it clearly, I myself something less.

As you know we always test fired our guns over the English Channel. Do you remember a ball turret gunner being shot to death while we were crossing the channel? In fact his body was splattered all over the ball turret. I can't remember whether the pilot aborted the mission or not, but I found out they had to wash out a lot of his remains from the turret so badly. Can you remember any of this.

Did Frank Harris tell you about the experiences they went through after they bailed out and were taken prisoners of war? One of the men lost a whole arm, shot off at the shoulder by flak. Another, a big chunk of meat shot off one of his arms. Harris himself had several vertebrae smashed beyond repair. This reminds me of how lucky we were when we flew "My Princess". I flew twenty four or twenty five missions in her and the only injury I got was a small piece of flak in my shoulder, and you got a small piece of flak in your little finger. I think we were extremely lucky, and to think that the very next crew that flew "My Princess" met with very unfortunate circumstances. It is something to think about. Frank said he weighed ninety pounds when he was liberated. I feel the same way that FDR stared one time, when he said, "War is hell".

There is one thing more about Sam Bell. Besides his own problem, he has a wife that has to have dialysis three times a week.

My gas tank is empty. Nice talking to you, till next time.

Radio to pilot, over and out.

James J. "Reddo" Redmond, Jr.

# LETTER NUMBER 28
JULY 12, 1999

Dear Lloyd:

I held off writing you until I could have copies made of the pictures I took at the reunion.

They turned out pretty good considering that I used one of those one time cameras. I have indicated the names of the people on the back of each picture.

There is one picture of Leonard Walline. I'm sure you can recognize him from the picture. (ha ha). He was difficult to talk to. He must have had some kind of a stroke. Some of his speech was very understandable, and some was difficult. It was not fun to talk to him.

I don't know whether we are talking about the same ball turret gunner who was shot over the channel. The understanding I retain was that the ball turret gunner was shot by tracer bullets. We were the only squadron using tracers that mission. The other squadrons were all using ammunition that did not include tracers. That meant that whoever shot him was a member of the 509th. I remember that he was shot in the back, but I don't remember the mess you described. I do seem to remember that this happened during test firing over the channel, but I have no recollection of who he was. Your recollections are probably accurate since they don't conflict in any way with mine.

One of the pictures is of Mike Hollingdale who lives near Polebrook. He knows Ken Crick very well. These men are members of" Friends of The Eighth Air Force" and are very active in keeping its memory alive. One of the men in the picture is Frank

Hatten. He was a 509th pilot who was being trained for group lead on a mission to Berlin. He was flying with Captain Clay, Squadron Operations Officer when just as we hit the IP their plane was hit and they had to leave the formation. There was some confusion when they left and we lost sight of the plane which was supposed to take over the lead. Since the whole group was behind me and following me, I took over the lead, continued on the bomb run and bombed Berlin. I rather doubt that you remember this because of your position in the plane. If you do, I would like to hear your recollections. Everybody from the front of the plane is now gone, so they can't contribute. Hatten and the other members of his crew were captured and were POWs for the remainder of the war.

I don't know if you had any knowledge of this or not, but if you do, comment on it. When we flew on "D" Day, it was Joe Berardi's and my thirtieth mission. We had plans to give the tower a buzz job that they would not soon forget. When it turned out to be "D" Day we decided it was not the thing to do. We figured there would be a second mission planned so we did not buzz the tower.

Then it was announced that there was no limit on combat tours. This of course pissed Berardi and me off completely. That night after dinner Berardi and I got a nose full at the Combat Officer's Club and decided to walk down to the Ground Gripper's Club and perhaps get nasty or at least obnoxious. I think we achieved both objectives. During our visit, I selected Col. Bob Burns (now General) and climbed all over him. I don't remember all that I said, but I can remember talking about how many missions I had flown without an abort and how many he and other administrative officers had flown. As I can remember he was very calm and tried to sooth me (and incidentally get the hell away from me.) Berardi had cornered Col. Romig, the base commander and was giving him hell. After we had satisfied ourselves that our feelings were established, we decided to leave. As we exited the front door, we spotted Col Romig's personal jeep parked in his personal parking place. Berardi said "Lets go inspect the guards". You may remember that there was suspicion that the Germans might drop paratroopers on the airfields to disrupt the air support for the invasion. Combat crews who had completed their tour were assigned to guard the planes and sound the alarm if there was any action. Anyway Berardi and I (Berardi was driving) roared out to the dispersal areas and roared from one plane to another inspecting the guards. The poor guards had to be nonplussed with two roaring drunk combat pilots in the Colonel's jeep, "inspecting the guard" When we inspected the last guard that we inspected, we could get no satisfaction. All he could do was laugh and say "Oh! wow, Lt. Redmond" over and over. I was too drunk to recognize him in the blackout, although I knew his voice. I later suspected he was a member of my crew, but I never found out. After completing the inspection of the guards we decided to check the main runway to make sure there were no Germans on it. We careened down the full length of the main runway several times at full throttle. I had all I could do to keep from falling out of the jeep. When Berardi was plastered, he was not a careful or a good driver. As a matter of fact we had a hard time staying on the runway. After the fun of our inspection trip we began to sober up a bit and decided to return the jeep. Berardi decided to take a short cut through a big mud puddle where we got stuck. It's hard to get a jeep stuck, but we did. We left the jeep in the middle of the large mud puddle and walked back to the barracks.

I wondered if that guard who laughed so much was a member of my crew or even if it might have been you. If you know anything about this, please tell me. I have wondered about it for a long time.

Pilot to radio, over and out.

Reddo

# LETTER NUMBER 29
AUGUST 1, 1999

Dear Reddo:

I was glad to get your letter and receive the pictures you took at the family reunion. I don't know why I said family. I had it typed before I could stop myself. Anyway they were good pictures. I enjoyed looking at them.

I can't say I remember Leonard Walline. His face doesn't ring a bell. After fifty five years I could have forgotten.

I wish I could be of more help about the mission to Berlin where you took over the lead after the lead plane got shot down. My position was the poorest position to see things going on.

There is one thing going on in my mind. The plane that we took over there, did we ever fly her in combat? I know we had three different planes we flew in combat. The first one was "Maggie's Drawers", the second was 'Snoozin Susan", and of course the last was "My Princess" Maybe you can tell me what the scoop is on this. I just plain can't remember.

You probably know that I correspond with Ken Crick. In fact I owe him a letter right now. I probably told you about him in one of my letters. He called when he was on vacation in Florida. It was difficult for me to understand him because of his cockney accent. When we were there I could understand their accent in fact I could imitate their accent pretty well. In my barracks it sounded more like s bunch of Limeys that it did American GIs.

No Reddo, that wasn't me wouldn't give you and Berardi the pass word when you were inspecting the guards, but kept laughing and saying, "Wow, Lt. Redmond" If it had been me I probably would have called you Reddo instead of Lt. Redmond. I never pulled any guard duty on any of the planes. I was aware of the scare that was out at the time about German paratroopers might try to land and disrupt things. The only guard duty I pulled while I was over there was after I finished my missions. I pulled guard duty for two weeks in a dugout on the outskirts of the air base with a fifty caliber water cooled machine gun. At that time all the enlisted men had to do this when they finished their tour of combat. Some of the guys walked a perimeter with a rifle over their shoulder. Sam Bell did the latter. He told me he cheated sometimes by leaving his post and going to get something to eat and drink. The punishment could have been severe if he had gotten caught. I'm not sure if anyone ever checked on us. Nobody ever checked on me.

I believe my wife is gradually getting better. She has gotten to the point where she can walk without aid of any kind and I'm so thankful. She had a bad experience. I've found out what kind of a person I am. It has made me a more patient person. I used to expect things to happen more quickly, but now I know some things take a little longer. It actually has made a better person out of me.

The picture of the memorial of the 351st that you sent me must have been made at Polebrook Air Force base. I have seen it before and I appreciate it. I still take great pride in being a part of such a great effort. My band and I take part every year in the fourth of July celebration at the Veterans Center here in Ardmore and have for the past several years. It still brings goose pimples up and down my spine when I let my mind go back to the actual time we were involved in our individual efforts as a crew, as a squadron, a group, a wing and the Eighth Air Force. I've been rewarded many different ways because I was a veteran and I', thankful for it. I wasn't drafted, I volunteered. After I finished my basic training the placement officer asked me what I would like to be, or what I would like to do while I was in the service. I said I would like to be a radio operator on a B-17. I got exactly what I wanted. It was hard for me to get used to flying, but I finally made the grade. You can testify to how hard it was for me to get used to flying. I thought I would never make it, but I did.

Years have a way of making you look old but as the saying goes, you are only as old as you think. You must be doing pretty good for yourself. Your picture shows you still looking good and in good health.

Did you tell me you are in marketing? I've been thinking about another business. I'm checking three different ones out. If any one of them works out, I'll let you know. As they say, this is a good life, but don't weaken.

There is a song, "If I had it to do all over again, I'd do it the same". I feel that way. As the words in the song go, I have no regrets. I have no excuses for the way I've lived my life. What you see is what you get. I guess I have blabbed long enough, but keep those letters coming, I enjoy them immensely.

Radio to pilot, over and out.

Lloyd

James J. "Reddo" Redmond, Jr.

# LETTER NUMBER 30
AUGUST 11, 1999

Dear Lloyd:

First of all, I'm sure glad that your wife is on the mend. I'm sure both of you will be glad to see her full recovery.

I did not expect you to remember Leonard Walline. He and his crew were there for only a short time before we were finished. He and his wife were nice people but we didn't have a lot to talk about.

Ken Crick's letters are easy to read because they are written in English, not cockney. Some of the English are difficult to understand: Mike Hollingdale who is a friend of Crick is quite easy to understand.

I talked with Sam Bell since my last letter to you and he has confirmed that he was on guard duty that night, and it is very possible that he was the guard who laughed. As I remember the voice, it seemed to be his.

The picture I sent you of the memorial was the one at Savannah. It is identical to the one at Polebrook.

I talked with Sam Bell about the time just before we were shipping out for combat. As you may remember I had my automobile with me at Alexandria. When we knew about when we would be leaving, I had to get my car back to Buffalo. I made arrangements with my parents to take a train to Memphis, where I would meet them, then drive back to Alexandria. After a few days they would take off for Buffalo. What I am getting at is; Sam Bell rode with me to Memphis along with Marty Strom, and I think two others. Sam had expected to meet an uncle there, but found out that he had a ruptured appendix operated on, then could not connect with some lady he knew. He rode back to Alexandria with me and my parents.

I remember the uncertainty of those days when we were about to go overseas. We had spent the last year preparing for combat and now we wondered if we were really ready. But ready or not, here we go.

I am going on vacation from August 18 to September 6. Will visit Buffalo and Youngstown. Keep safe and healthy and keep your wife on the road to recovery.

Pilot to radio, over and out.

Reddo

*James J. "Reddo" Redmond, Jr.*

# LETTER NUMBER 31
SEPTEMBER 10, 1999

Dear Reddo:

I'm a little late about answering your letter but I've been a little busy trying to get a business going: laying the foundation.

Was glad to get your letter. I hope your trip was an enjoyable one. I don't believe you said whether you were going to drive your car or not. If you did that's a lot of driving. Your home was in New York someplace when we were overseas. Was the city Buffalo? I'm not sure.

I'm sure glad this hot weather has let up for at least a while. It was getting me down. I didn't seem to have any pep. Me and hot weather don't seem to get along very well.

I believe you told me you were in marketing. That's what I'm trying to get started. I want to get into something. I thought about commodities, but have given up on it for a while. I'm not too familiar with it yet. I have taken a course in it, but there's a lot to it. A broker has promised to help me get started by paper trading at first. (not real money) It is something you can lose your shirt on if you don't know what your doing. I'll have to do some more thinking on this.

I'll be going to our yearly family reunion on the 19th of this month. It has been going on for years. It's held in the city i grew up in. A place called Hanna on the western end of Lake Eufaula. The lake wasn't there when I was growing up.

I've got a birthday coming up on October 24th. I'll be 78 years young. When is your birthday? These years keep flying by. What do you think is going to happen in the year 2000? I think something is going to happen but I'm not sure what.

Sam Bell is a nice fellow to talk to, isn't he? I've talked to him twice and found him to be an engaging fellow to talk to. He told me a lot of things I didn't know about. After we came back from overseas he and Wes Creech were stationed together at Amarillo. Creech's wife was a good looking woman, I thought, and this is where the trouble began. According to Bell, the guys at the base began taking notice of her, and I guess she couldn't resist. It was fascinating to me to hear Bell talk about it. I think Creech and I were the only married men on the crew while we were overseas, am I right?

I've got a niece that lives in Ft. Lauderdale but I don't know who she married, which doesn't help much.

Keep the letters coming because I love to hear from you very much. I missed one edition of the Polebrook Post. This makes twice this has happened. I hope its the last. I've got to go.

Radio to pilot, over and out.

Lloyd

James J. "Reddo" Redmond, Jr.

# LETTER NUMBER 32
OCTOBER 1, 1999

Dear Lloyd:

There's not a lot happening here, but I wanted to get back to you about trading in commodities. This is a treacherous business and not intended for amateurs. In thirty or sixty days you can lose your entire investment. Of course the brokers want all the sacrificial lambs they can find, because the make money each time you trade, whether you win or lose.

The only way to get into this business is to do it like Hillary Clinton did. She had brokers who back dated her transactions so that she couldn't lose money. You remember she traded $1,000.00 into $100,000.00. This was no accident. For the $100,000.00 she made, some poor sucker or group of suckers lost $100,000.00. This game is only for those who can afford to lose whatever hey invest with out thinking about it. If you are in that class, then go ahead and have fun. I have listened to these brokers advertise futures and commodity trading and it sure looks attractive. Any way, forewarned is forearmed.

I'll bet you had a good time at your family reunion. Tell me all about it. Our family reunion is next year (2000) in Soldotna, Alaska. We have relatives there. Our last reunion was five years ago in Buffalo, N.Y.

Yes the years go by faster and faster. I'll be eighty next August 25th. Because of that I am giving thought to attending the next 351st Bomb Group reunion in Polebrook, England. Why don't you give some thought to this? You know you are not getting any younger and in a few years you won't be capable of going. I have written to Joe Berardi a pilot who went through training with me (all through cadets and phase training) and was in the 509th squadron of the 351st Bomb Group and suggested he attend. He lives in Reading Pa. and came to visit when I visited my daughter in Buffalo.

For something to do, why not look in the yellow pages under Market Research. Then call and see if they can use you. You won't make a lot of money, but then you won't chance losing a bunch of money. A last word of advice, don't get into any business unless you know all about it. If you do, it's a sure was to lose both your shirt and pants, and maybe your underwear.

Let me know what happens.

Pilot to radio, over and out.

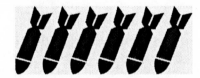

Correspondence between Reddo Redmond and Lloyd Bogle continues to the present day, but the recollections of, and references to our war time experiences seem to have run their course. Therefore, although it may seem abrupt, I have decided to terminate this collection of letters before they lost their pertinence.

# SECTION THREE: Ancillaries, Vignettes And Combat Statistics Supplementing The Three Preceding Sections

The various items which make up this section, while not a direct part of combat, will help to understand a number of things which the combat crews encountered during their tour. Also included are a few poems and passages relating to aerial combat, as well as some statistics documenting the casualty rates experienced by the combat crews.

Generally speaking, for the combat crew, life went on in a manner not too dissimilar to life in the States during the periods when they were not in combat. However, there were some differences which were not helped by the commonality of language. These will be treated separately because they are so different from each other.

## THE SHOWER

When the 351st Bomb Group arrived in England, they took possession of an existing RAF Base at Polebrook. This base had been built and designed to suit the requirements of the English. The English did not have much interest in the shower which they called "The Sprinkle." When the English thought it was necessary, or desirable, they took a bath not a shower.

Since the Americans could not exist without a shower, the English agreed to construct shower facilities. They proceeded to construct a separate building for the showers. Like most construction in England, it was built to last. It was made of concrete. It had two bays and each bay had about twelve shower heads delivering water from directly above. These were communal (no booths). The water came straight down and it was impossible to shower without soaking your hair. The on/off knob was a single control such as is on a garden hose faucet. This did not control hot/cold water temperature. When the water was turned on, it was freezing cold then it went from cold, through warm, to scalding hot. The procedure we first adopted was to turn on one shower, wait till the water was warm, jump in, get wet and move out before the water got too hot. Then go to the next shower and repeat the procedure until you were finished. Then some one made an amazing discovery. There was a mixing valve somewhere that provided a nice temperature water if all the showers were turned on. This must have used hundreds of gallons of water for one person to shower and the Ministry of Water Conservation was always bitching about the water usage. There was no heat in this building. It had a stove but it was never attended. In the winter months, the free air temperature was about fifty degrees.

## THE BATH

In America, a bath room consists of a proper sized room containing a bath tub, a toilet, and a wash stand with mirrors. In England, at least at our base, a bath room is exactly what the name infers. It contains a bath tub and nothing else. The bath rooms at our base were part of the original facilities on the base which we took over from the RAF.

An English bath tub is different from an American bath tub. An American bath tub is relatively short and wide. It is necessary to sit up in an American bath tub. Not so with an English bath tub. They are long and narrow. It is possible to lay down almost full length in an English bath tub.

Since there were no heating facilities, the room temperature would be whatever the outside temperature was. In the winter months, usually about fifty degrees. The American combat crews would sometimes take a bath to relax after a difficult mission. When taking a bath, you would get the tub filled with comfortably warm water and then get submerged up to your neck. As you became accustomed to the temperature of the water, you would keep adding more hot water until the temperature of the water would be well over 100 degrees. When it was time to get out, it took a real act of courage. When the water drained off and the cold air hit you, it felt like some one was shooting icicles at you or you were at the North Pole. You would towel off quickly, dress and take the half mile walk to the barracks.

## HOTELS

It seems that many of our recollections have to do with being cold. I don't think that any of the hotels had central heat, at least in the bedrooms. I know that none of those I patronized did. The temperature of the room would be somewhere near the outside temperature. However, every room had its own little gas heating stove. These were coin operated and they accepted only pennies. Each penny deposited delivered a certain number of minutes of gas service. When the service paid for by the deposited pennies is used up, the fire goes out. Most Americans had plenty of change and if there were two of you, the pennies are pooled. Newly arrived Americans not understanding the use of the stoves would deposit all their pennies in the stove and go to bed in a comfortable room. However, during the night all the pennies would be used up and the gas stove would pop off. The next morning it was freezing in the room, and since you had used up all your pennies, you had no way to heat it. After an experience with the stove, everyone would remember to save a few pennies for the morning.

## THE BLACK OUT

America had some black out drills when there was fear that the Japanese would bomb us, but the people did not really take these seriously. The American black out produced only a slight

226

darkening of the area. The English black out produced a complete lack of illumination so that practically nothing was visible.

My first experience with the black out came when we landed at Nuts Corners, a suburb of Belfast in Northern Ireland. My co-pilot and I changed our American money into British pounds, shillings and pence, and decided to see Belfast. We had no idea of the value of the British money and when we boarded the bus for Belfast, I offered the driver a half crown (this looks like an American half dollar). The driver said "Blimy, governor, aven't you anything smaller?" I showed him my handful of change and he picked out three pennies.

We asked him to let us know when we got to the down town section and he replied that it was at the end of the line. It had gotten dark while traveling to town and when we got off the bus we found ourselves standing on the sidewalk all alone. The bus had gone and it was pitch black. There were pedestrians hurrying to and fro. We could see them because most of them were carrying torches (flash lights). We stopped one of them and asked her where was downtown. She told us it was one block over. As we walked, I suddenly discovered that I was not getting any response to my conversation. My co-pilot had drifted about fifteen feet away. It was so dark that I could not see him. We spent the rest of the evening walking, holding hands. We probably made a very pretty picture.

When we arrived at the down town section of Belfast, you could see nothing at all. There was no illumination. If you did not know where something was, you could not find it. When someone would open a door to enter a building you could see a brief flash of light. We gained entry to a number of places by entering as soon as we saw a flash of light that was close enough for us to follow. We found our way into a variety of places, including a private home, a boarding house, a pub and a hotel. We had a few at the pub and then put up at the hotel. While we were in the lobby of the hotel an attractive girl approached the desk clerk and asked him to "please knock me up at eight". We came to attention, but she had gone upstairs and an international incident was avoided. We later found out that was the British way of leaving a wake up call.

On a subsequent visit to Belfast we were unable to locate the girl who had expressed a desire to be "knocked up at eight." Given an opportunity we were all anxious to accommodate. This was not the only British expression to cause wonderment and consternation to newly arrived Americans. We had just become acquainted with some ladies, with promises to get together the next day. On saying good by, the last comment by the ladies was "Keep your pecker up." As worldly and sophisticated as we thought we were, we were floored. We subsequently found out that this phrase means "Keep your spirits up."

## BELFAST TAXI CABS

Remembering our experience with the black out, we decided we had better not mess with the bus system. We would take a taxi cab back to the base. We approached the first cab we saw and the driver agreed to take us to the air base. First he would have to go back to his station and get a full load of gas. He did not mean gasoline or petrol. His cab ran on some kind of bottle gas that was pumped into a huge canvas bag strapped to the top of the cab.

The bag looked like a small dirigible or blimp. It was larger than the cab. When we left for the air base it was big, full and round. As we went through the country side we could see the shadow of the cab and the bag reflected in the ditch. The farther we traveled the emptier the bag got until it was flapping in the breeze. When we arrived at the air base the bag was flat. It was empty of gas. We felt sorry for the driver and asked him how he would get back to Belfast. He said he would get a push. I don't know who he would get a push from, but the next evening he was gone. We tipped him pretty good so he was not too upset. Subsequently, whenever we wanted a taxi cab to take us to the air base it was necessary to find a petrol cab, the gas bag cabs would not take us.

## ENGLISH BUSSES

Most of the busses were of the double deck variety. I don't remember whether the engine was in the front or the rear of the bus, but this was not significant to this feature. In England, during the war, petrol or gasoline was in very short supply, so the bus engines were converted to run on a gas vapor similar to that used by the Belfast taxi cabs. This gas was produced by a coke stove or a small furnace. While it may sound unreasonable to combine a furnace with a bus, the English solved the problem this way. A platform was built on the rear of the bus where the rear bumper would be. On the platform they placed a small coke furnace with some equipment to produce the gas vapor and deliver it to the engine. The busses seemed to operate very well on this fuel, but it was necessary for the driver or perhaps the conductor to periodically stop, go back to the stove, shake out the ashes and add more fuel. The driver would then get back in the bus and continue the run. In this manner, bus service was maintained in good fashion, however, it did seem strange to an American to see the driver get off the bus and tend the furnace.

## CANDY

Candy was a real treat. We were allowed two nickel candy bars a week. Of course this did not include the ration received for combat missions when each combat crew member received one candy bar, two cookies and a pack of gum. When ration day arrived, much deliberation was required to select from a very frugal selection. The selection made was usually a chocolate bar for taste and a candy that could be sucked so it would last longer. We often remembered our foolishness in eating all the candy we brought to England.

We savored the candy while we were in England, I guess because of its scarcity and when we boarded the ocean liner to return to the States we found there was a ships store where candy could be purchased. Several of us went to see if we could buy a candy bar. We were startled to find out we could not buy a candy bar - we had to buy a carton of them. Once we had a carton of candy bars in the cabin, the longing for them no longer existed. It was the old story that when something is scarce it becomes very valuable and when it becomes plentiful, its value fades.

## CHRISTMAS 1943

We had completed a long and exciting journey from our final training base in Alexandria, Louisiana to our new base in Polebrook, England.  This is where we will be permanently stationed for our combat tour.  During our first days at Polebrook we did not have very much to do.  There was very little combat flying because the Eighth Air Force had been restricted from long missions into Germany.  This restriction was imposed during the period from late October 1943 to mid January 1944, while headquarters considered scrapping the entire daylight bombing campaign.  This matter had to be considered in view of the combat losses running in excess of twenty percent on missions to Schweinfurt and Regensburg on Black Thursday.

**Midnight Mass at Polebrook**

The morale of the combat crews was not very high and by the time Christmas arrived, the crew was not in the best of spirits. There was nostalgia for Christmases past and a feeling of depression brought about by a period of little activity, after living a life of dynamic activity.

When we were at Goose Bay, Labrador on our way to England, I had an opportunity to buy a bottle of liquor.  I don't know why I bought it.  I was not a liquor drinker I was a beer drinker.  It was a lucky thing that I bought the liquor, because on Christmas Day I got the crew together, produced the bottle, and we had a party. All feelings of depression flew out the window (right through the black out curtains). We had lots of fruit juice to mix with the liquor from the batch we lugged from Goose Bay. I actually had forgotten this occurrence until Lloyd Bogle mentioned it to me.

## THE RACCOON FRATERNITY

In flying combat, in addition to your heated clothing and protective gear, it was necessary to wear an oxygen mask, goggles, a fleece lined leather helmet ear phones and a steel helmet. The free air temperature could be as cold as seventy degrees below zero (the coldest temperature I saw was seventy two degrees below zero). The temperature in the cockpit would range well below zero. The gunners in the waist and rear of the plane were subject to severe cold because their guns required open windows in order to operate. It seems like a contradiction that your body and its extremes could be so cold that feeling would be lost and at the same time you could be sweating profusely. In the heat of battle, it often happened that sweat from your forehead would roll down and freeze on the oxygen mask. The debris from the sweat and dirt would mark your face so that when you removed the oxygen mask and goggles you looked just like a bandit raccoon. The dirt marks could be washed off, but the lines left by the oxygen mask and the goggles remained until after a nights sleep.

## OXYGEN MASK ICICLES

This phenomenon is peculiar only to the pilot. In flying the close formation required in the combat box, the pilot must fly for long periods without changing the position of his head. The breath being discharged from the oxygen mask condenses and freezes forming an icicle running from the oxygen mask to the seat belt. If you had occasion to turn your head, the icicle would break off and drop into your lap. If it was not disturbed it would melt as you descended into warmer temperatures. Many pilots flew an entire tour never becoming aware of this phenomenon if the icicle melted before they had occasion to move their head and break the icicle.

## FLAK SUITS

Each combat crew member was provided with a flak suit. A flak suit was a garment that was to be worn as an over the head apron. It was made of overlapping pieces of metal designed to deflect flak shrapnel. The gunners who spent most of their time in a standing position could wear these without a lot of discomfort despite their weight. The gunners in other positions modified their use to accommodate their requirements. For me as pilot, the flak suit was far too heavy and bulky to wear in any of the approved positions. I took the apron of the suit which was rectangular in shape and laid it across my lap with the corner protecting my chest. It never deflected a shot, but it gave me a feeling of security. My crew chief, Ed Kurek, fashioned a piece of armor plating to position underneath my seat cushion. These two items gave me all the protection available. The ball turret operator was in such small and cramped quarters that he did not have a choice of wearing a flak suit or not. All he had room for was the clothing to keep him warm.

## LONDON AFTER THE BLITZ

Much of London had been destroyed during the blitz in 1940 and 1941. Whole city blocks had been leveled. Now two years after the blitz, the rubble had been cleared up and carted away, but whole city blocks which were leveled bore mute testimony to the destruction and terror the city and its citizens had undergone.

As bad as the observable destruction was, the real tragedy was felt by the citizens who lost loved ones, their homes and belongings. It was a real problem for these homeless people to find a place to sleep. They took over the tube (subway). I don't know if this was an official program or whether the homeless Londoners just saw the facility and moved in. During the daytime hours on every level of every station, personal belongings of the homeless would be neatly bundled and stacked against the walls. These little bundles contained all their worldly possessions. Their homes and all their belongings had been destroyed in the blitz. The people had to get out and do whatever they did during the day. About nine o'clock at night, they would appear again and make up their bed (probably a blanket) and prepare to sleep on the steel or concrete floor. They didn't bother anyone and the passengers didn't bother them. At midnight all trains stopped running and the tube was quiet. As quiet as thousands of people would be. It was pathetic, but this was something the English tolerated rather than submit to Hitler.

All public transportation stopped at midnight. There were no busses, taxicabs or subway. If you were a long way from where you wanted to be for the night, the only route available was walking. This happened to me once. I had to walk about four or five miles. This never happened to me again.

## THE TWENTY FIVE MISSION COMBAT TOUR

When the Air Offensive Europe was commenced by the Eighth Air Force, it was considered that twenty-five missions was the maximum number of missions that a combat crew man could survive before he would be in danger of cracking up.

When General James Doolittle was appointed to command the Eighth Air Force, in the spring of 1944 he increased the tour to thirty missions. This caused great consternation among the combat crews. The expression that reflected the morale and attitude of the combat crews was, "If you get shot down before you completed twenty-five missions, you don't have to do the extra five."

There was a great amount of bitching and loud protestations by the crews that they would not do the extra five missions, but when push came to shove, all just kept on flying, hoping to complete thirty.

There was a feeling among many of the combat crews that after they had completed twenty-five missions, they had used up their luck and were flying on borrowed time. This proved to be true for many of them, because many were shot down after they had completed twenty-five missions, and before they completed thirty.

*James J. "Reddo" Redmond, Jr.*

For my part, I had about ten or eleven missions completed when the increase to thirty was announced. Although I was browned off (British expression), I adjusted to the new tour and considered my tour to be thirty missions.

I flew my thirtieth mission on "D" Day, June 6, 1944. I thought I had reached the unreachable and had completed my tour. I was wrong. It was announced that because of the uncertainty that the invasion would succeed, there would be no tour limit. During the month of June 1944, I flew four more missions. It is hard to explain, even though these missions were comparatively easy, I experienced an uneasy feeling that I had used up my luck. After I had completed my thirty-fourth mission, it was announced that anyone who had completed thirty missions on "D" Day was finished.

This announcement was made at lunch time after we had returned from a mission. This was the second time I thought I had completed my tour. The first time I had been elated, I thought I had accomplished the impossible. This time I did not feel the elation. I felt let down. The knowledge that I was finished was so anti climactic, that I didn't really know how I felt. A factor that entered into my feelings was the fact that I was no longer a combat crew man. I would no longer share the concerns and fears of those who would continue flying combat.

## GERMAN JETS AND ROCKETS

I vividly remember several things which were not included in the descriptions of the combat missions. I did not make record of them and therefore cannot ascribe them to specific missions. I think these incidents are note worthy and I will describe them here.

The German Jet, ME 262 which did not become operational until late 1944, was such a performer that allied fighter planes could not compete with it. On a few missions where American B-17 formations were attacked by ME 262s the result for the Americans was disastrous. The P-51s could only down the ME262 by attacking them as they were on landing approach. There is serious concern whether we could have won the war if the ME262 had become operational six months sooner.

The ME262 never attacked a formation in which I was flying. However, I did see one that must have been on a test flight. To me it seemed to be going straight up at a terrific rate of speed. It went by so fast that I was not sure what I had seen. Discussions with others who had been on that mission confirmed my observations.

On another mission, what must have been a rocket (or a surface to air missile) shot up from the ground and passed my left wing, going straight up. It was very close to us because we cut through the contrail almost immediately. All of this happened so fast that I did not see the rocket, only the contrail. If you weren't looking right at the spot where the rocket went by, you probably wouldn't see anything. Discussions back at the base did not produce any one who had seen it. I saw it and my co-pilot, Frank Cavanaugh saw it. I never saw another one, but this one was for real.

Another incident which I did not record in my diaries but which is worthy of mention here is concerned with the performance of an American fighter pilot. We were supposed to have fighter escort on this mission, but we had not seen them and were not sure where they were. This was during the time when the American fighter pilots were authorized to get down on the deck and destroy anything they could. Suddenly, we discovered four twin engine German fighter bombers queuing up in echelon formation and preparing to lob rockets at us from the side of the formation out of range of our fifty caliber machine guns. Since we were supposed to have an escort, someone called for assistance and one fighter pilot answered, "I'll be right there." As we observed the German planes fixing to get into position, we could see one American Fighter behind them and much lower, climbing to gain altitude. Finally, he had altitude above and behind them. The Germans still had no idea that he was there. He started to dive and shot down the last German plane before the other three even knew anything was happening. Then in quick order, he shot down the remaining three, all in one pass. It was necessary for him to chase the last one a long distance as the German attempted to dive away. The combat crew men in the bombers were amazed at this performance. We called and thanked him, and he replied "OK is there anything else around?' We responded "No", and he answered, "Call me if you see any thing" and he dove for the deck where I guess he was having fun.

At de-briefing, all the crews that observed this were reporting it and a reporter from the newspaper "Stars and Stripes" heard it and investigated. Two days later Stars and Stripes had an article describing this incident and reported that the American fighter pilot was a brand new combat pilot on his first mission. He was credited with four kills. He was in combat only a few hours and he was almost an Ace.

I do not remember on which missions these occurrences took place so they are reported here separately. All three happened in late spring 1944.

## CRITIQUE

A critique was a meeting held, usually after four or five missions, during which the performance of the group in combat was discussed. A critique might be held after a single mission if that mission was particularly disastrous. These meetings were usually very embarrassing for those officers who had screwed up, although they did clarify and solve problems discussed. As an example, at one of the group critiques there was the instance when the pilot of a crew on their first mission aborted the mission and returned to the base without entering enemy territory. His reason for aborting the mission was deemed not of sufficient seriousness to abort the mission. In the presence of the entire group, he was called upon to explain his reasoning. After he had done so, the comment from the Colonel conducting the critique was that the pilot had the usual shit storm normal to a first mission. He would be demoted from Aircraft commander to co-pilot until he demonstrated his ability to execute the responsibilities of an aircraft commander.

These were rough times in a rough business. The reason an abort was so serious was that the absence of an airplane from the formation left that place vacant without the protection of its thirteen guns. The integrity of the group was violated and the entire group was endangered by the absence of that one plane. In flying thirty four missions, I never aborted once, even though there were a number of times when I considered it. Most aborts are caused by mechanical failure. Our never having aborted demonstrates the quality of maintenance provided by our ground crew chief Sgt. Ed Kurek and his men. There were few pilots or crew chiefs who could make this claim.

## ENEMY FIGHTERS VERSUS FLAK

There have been many arguments as to which enemy activity was the most devastating and frightening. This argument will never be settled so long as there is any one alive who faced either or both of these features of combat.

Those who flew missions before "D" Day faced the Lufftwaffe at its deadliest and severe flak barrages at the target. Those who flew missions after "D" Day did not encounter German fighters in any appreciable numbers because the Lufftwaffe had been destroyed by the advent of the P-51 in combat. They faced more intense flak barrages at the target as the Germans improved and increased their protection around targets.

For my part, having faced both flak and enemy fighters at full strength, I would prefer to circle in a flak barrage than face a determined attack by a substantial fighter group.

All of the above is a matter of personal opinion, since whatever force you faced will seem to be the worst.

*James J. "Reddo" Redmond, Jr.*

## FIGHTER ESCORT

When the Eighth Air Force first began to fly combat missions out of England over the continent, it was believed that the B-17, Flying Fortress was so heavily armed with 50 Caliber machine guns that it could defend itself against any fighter attacks the Germans could mount.

The first combat efforts of the Eighth Air Force were flown with no escort at all. The results were catastrophic. It was recognized that the bombers needed help. After a few missions, escort was provided by the RAF with their Spitfires. However, the Spitfires had been designed and built for the Battle of Britain and had very little range. The Spitfires could only accompany the bombers for a short distance when they had to leave the bombers and return to England. Early 1944 saw the arrival of both the P-47 and the P-38. They were put into service escorting the bombers. While their range was much longer than that of the Spitfire, they could still only go part way with the bombers. Rather than mix with the American fighters, the Germans would wait until the escorting fighters had exhausted their fuel and left the bombers. Then they would attack. The battle would last all the way to the target, and then all the way back to where escort fighters could again provide protection.

The losses suffered by bombers without escort were so severe - amounting to twenty percent of participating bombers that only a few such missions would have wiped out the Eighth Air Force. The situation was so serious that from October 1943 to February 1944 no long range missions into Germany were flown. Serious consideration was being given to canceling the entire program of daylight bombing.

In the spring of 1944, wing tanks were added to the American fighters to extend their range and the American P-51 arrived to fly escort. The P-51 with wing tanks could go anywhere the bombers could. (A wing tank is a fuel tank suspended under the wing of a fighter which would be jettisoned when going into action.) When escort could be provided all the way to the target and back, the bombing program became viable.

The bomber crews felt an emotion toward the escort fighters that is impossible to describe. When we came under attack and the escort fighters dropped their wing tanks and speeded up to the attack I felt a sensation such as a kid experiences when his big brother appears to help in a fight which is going badly. Without the long range American fighters such as the P-51, the Eighth Air Force could not have survived long range missions.

The arrival of the P-51 in combat was not without problems. The P-51 was new to combat and its pilots were also new to combat and escort service to the bombers. The P-51 pilots, being new, did not appreciate how difficult it was for the bomber crews to differentiate between the German ME-109 and the P-51. The preferred method of attack by the Germans was head on and they would press their attack to the extent that they flew right through the bomber formation. The new P-51 pilots, chasing the ME-109s, would follow the Germans right through the bomber formation.

Everyone would be shooting: the Germans, the P-51s and the bomber crews. It was said that the P-51s downed some bombers and the bomber crews downed some P-51s and both the bomber crews and the P-51s downed some Germans and the Germans shot down some B-17s and P-51s. After this mix-up, the P-51 pilots learned that the bomber crews fired at any plane that pointed its nose at them. Before joining a bomber group for escort, the P-51s now made a real effort to display their profile so that the bomber crews knew that these were P-51s.

## FIRST THERE WERE TOILETS AND THEN THERE WAS TOILET PAPER
Since the subject of shower facilities and the English bath tub have been discussed separately, it may be appropriate to mention an item known as bath tissue, or as more commonly called, toilet paper.

The English suffered severely from shortages of almost every thing needed to keep a civilization functioning. Our calling attention to this seemingly unimportant item is less to chastise them that it is to complement them in their solution of a minor problem which affected millions of people.

I have no awareness of the problems faced by the government in producing sufficient toilet paper to handle the needs of the populace. I am only aware of the product which seemed to be in universal use.

The paper which was in use in facilities available to the public, had a consistency somewhat akin to waxed paper. When the paper was folded around one's hand, rather than smoothly following the contours of the hand, it crinkled itself into a number of sharp points, which added nothing to the comfort in accomplishing the final function of the paper. No one would, of course, ascribe this feature of the paper to the government's desire to conserve all resources. Nevertheless, it did result in limiting its use to as few sheets as possible.

The poor British had no alternative but to use this paper. Whereas we Americans were supplied with American G.I. Issue, and although we may have been critical when State side, we found nothing wrong with it in the British Isles. Any time I expected to be away from the Base for a length of time, I always managed to bring an adequate supply of G.I. toilet paper.

## SEXY NONSENSE IN THE STATES
This episode happened just prior to our departure for England, but I thought it deserved inclusion in the story of our crew.

It so happened that as the time for us to go overseas and into combat drew near; we were all possessed of a recklessness that had not been experienced previously. At our base in Alexandria Louisiana, the shower rooms were located about twenty yards from the B.O.Q.(Bachelor Officer's Quarters). The trip to and from the showers was accomplished with only a towel wrapped around the waist. Additional wrap was not needed because the weather was mild.

The nurse's quarters were located about forty or fifty yards from the path between the BOQ and the showers. Shift time for the nurses leaving the hospital to return to their quarters coincided with our shower time in the late afternoon preparatory to going into town. The base bus would drop a group of nurses at a stop where they would walk within forty or fifty yards of our path to the showers. It seemed to happen that frequently we would be returning from the shower to the BOQ as the nurses were returning to quarters.

This whole affair started when some of the nurses began to cheer us as though we were part of a performance. In our reckless state, very little encouragement was needed to induce us to perform a sort of fan dance with our towels, and the nurses would cheer us on. After a few dances, we would end our dance by flipping our towel over our shoulder, stand there for a brief second, and then take off for the BOQ. The nurses would hoot and holler as we exited.

This dance performance was only performed by Bud Ritzema, pilot of another crew, Marty Strom, my navigator, and me. We thought our dance was a fitting farewell to the USA as we prepared to leave for combat. Bud Ritzema was shot down on his first mission.

## BOGLE'S SECRET WEAPON
One occurrence which gave the crew a real belly laugh happened when Lloyd Bogle, in his cramped radio room, was maneuvering around trying to get a shot at an enemy fighter when his parachute harness caught on the release lever for one of the dingys to be used when ditching. The dingy was released and flew down the side of the plane, inflating as it went until it smashed into Palmer's side window. Palmer thought the plane had been destroyed and was ready to bail out, but the other crew men

*James J. "Reddo" Redmond, Jr.*

calmed him down.  This was later referred to as "Bogle's Secret Weapon."

# MISSIONS AND LOSSES

Following is a listing of the 34 combat missions flown by Reddo's Raiders together with the name of the target and the number of heavy bombers lost by the Eighth Air Force on each mission.

| DATE 1944 | TARGET | Bombers Lost |
|---|---|---|
| 2/6 | Caen, France | 6 |
| 2/21 | Leipzig, Germany | 25 |
| 2/21 | Achmer, Germany | 23 |
| 2/24 | Scweinfurt, Germany | 46 |
| 3/3 | Wilhelmshaven, Germany | 14 |
| 3/4 | Bonn, Germany | 16 |
| 3/8 | Erkner, Germany | 40 |
| 3/9 | Berlin, Germany | 69 |
| 3/11 | Munster, Germany | 29 |
| 3/20 | Frankfurt, Germany | 8 |
| 3/22 | Berlin, Germany | 13 |
| 3/23 | Munster, Germany | 29 |
| 3/24 | Schweinfurt, Germany | 8 |
| 3/26 | Watten, France | 6 |
| 3/27 | Tours, France | 11 |
| 3/29 | Braunschweig, Germany | 10 |
| 4/11 | Arnswalde, Germany | 69 |
| 4/19 | Kassel, Germany | 6 |
| 4/20 | No Ball, France | 15 |
| 4/22 | Hamm, Germany | 30 |
| 4/24 | Erding, Germany | 55 |
| 5/7 | Berlin, Germany | 13 |
| 5/9 | Luxenburg, Germany | 10 |
| 5/11 | Luxenburg, Germany | 13 |
| 5/12 | Meiseburg, Germany | 55 |

| 5/22 | Kiel, Germany | 7 |
| 5/24 | Berlin, Germany | 34 |
| 5/25 | Metz, France | 6 |
| 5/27 | Ludwigshaven, Germany | 32 |
| 6/6 | Invasion Coast, Normandy, France | 6 "D" Day |
| 6/11 | Bernay St. Martin, France | 5 |
| 6/12 | Cambrai, France | 17 |
| 6/14 | Paris, France | 19 |
| 6/20 | Hamburg | 50 |
| | TOTAL: | 849 |

Sources: Combat Chronology 1941 - 1945- Authors Kit Carter and Robert Mueller, Center for Air Force History.
Mighty Eighth War Diary, Author, Roger A. Freeman.

# TWO WRITINGS OF COL. BUDD PEASLEE, COMMANDER OF THE 384TH BOMB GROUP

### ONE: HELPLESSNESS

A description of the feeling of utter helplessness that plagued the bomber crews as their cumbersome craft seemed to crawl across the skies toward the target.

"I think of the middle ages. I see myself strolling across an open plain with a group of friends. Suddenly we are beset by many scoundrels on horseback. They come from every direction, shooting their arrows. We defend ourselves as best we can with slings and swords and crouch behind our leather shields. We cannot dodge, we cannot hide. The plain has no growth, no rocks, no holes. And it seems endless, there is no way out—then or now"

The foregoing writing from Col. Budd Peaslee describes better than I, the feelings that are experienced when under attack. You have no choice. Your route is straight ahead to the target regardless of the hazards being encountered.

Realizing the feelings described above makes even more impressive the fact that in all of the Air Offensive, no Eighth Air Force mission was ever turned back by enemy action.

## TWO: TO CONCLUDE THE CENTURY

"The tumult and the shouting have died away. The B-17s and B-24s will never again assemble into strike formation in the bitter cold of embattled skies. Never again will the musical thunder of their passage cause the very earth to tremble. The source of sound lost in infinity and seeming to emanate from all things, visible and invisible. The great deep throated engines are forever silent, replaced by the flat toneless roar of the jets and rockets. But on bleak and lonely winter nights in the English Midlands, ghost squadrons take off silently in the swirling mists of the North Sea from the ancient weed choked runways. They wing away toward the east, never to return. On other nights the deserted woodlands ring with unheard laughter and gay voices of young men and women who once passed that way. Recollections of all these fade a little with each passing year until at last there will finally remain only the indelible records of the All Seeing Master of the Universe to recall the deeds of valor excelled by no other nation, arm or service. These sacred scrolls will forever remain the heritage of the free and untrammeled people of this earth."

*James J. "Reddo" Redmond, Jr.*

# COMBAT EXPERIENCE OF THE 351ST BOMB GROUP

In the descriptions of the combat missions in which Reddo's Raiders participated in, there are frequent references and intimations of how difficult it was to complete a combat tour. In some instances there were direct descriptions of the terror encountered in combat. The following chart shows what happened to the planes of the 351st Bomb Group in the Air Offensive, Europe.

**Total number of B-17s assigned to the 351st was**        **280**

Disposition:

| | | |
|---|---|---|
| Missing in action (shot down) | 104 | |
| Crashed on return from Combat | 20 | |
| Scrapped due to battle damage | 30 | |
| Ditched in the English Channel | 13 | |
| Destroyed in collision over England | 5 | |
| Landed or crashed in neutral countries | 8 | |
| Transferred to other Groups | 24 | |
| Returned to USA | 76 | **280** |

**Total B-17s lost due to enemy action in combat**      **175**

During the Air Offensive over Europe, six thousand five hundred thirty-three (6,533) heavy bombers and their crews were lost by the Eighth Air Force due to enemy action.

The total KIA (Killed in action) of the Eighth Air Force almost equals the total KIA of the U.S. Navy and U.S. Marines combined, and one out of ten Americans killed in World War II was a combat crew man of the Eighth Air Force.

The 351st Bomb Group flew 311 combat missions over occupied Europe between 1943 and 1945. One hundred seventy five B-17 Flying Fortresses and their crews were lost and 303 enemy aircraft were destroyed in aerial combat.

Sources: Combat Chronology 1941 - 1945- Authors Kit Carter and Robert Mueller, Center for Air Force History.
Mighty Eighth War Diary, Author, Roger A. Freeman.

# LIFE EXPECTANCY OF A B-17 OF THE 351st BOMB GROUP

From the activation of the 351st in April 1943 to "D" Day in 1944:

14 B-17s were lost on their first mission
30 B-17s were lost before their 10th mission
40 B-17s were lost between their 11th and 25th missions
<u>26</u> B-17s were lost after having flown more than 25 missions
120 TOTAL

From "D" Day to the end of operations of the 351st on April 20, 1945:

0 B-17s were lost on their first mission
17 B-17s were lost before their 10th mission
17 B-17s were lost between their 11th and 25th mission
<u>27</u> B-17s were lost after having flown more than 25 missions
61 TOTAL

181 B-17s lost in combat by the 351st Bomb Group

The above schedules refer only to airplanes, not combat crews, since crews frequently flew a variety of planes. The variance in totals of lost planes can be explained by the different interpretation of the category of planes destroyed in collision over England.

# EIGHTH AIR FORCE HEAVY BOMBER LOSSES BY MONTH 1942-1945

| **1942** | |
|---|---|
| August | 2 |
| September | 3 |
| October | 12 |
| November | 13 |
| December | 20 |
| | 50 |

| **1943** | |
|---|---|
| January | 20 |
| February | 38 |
| March | 24 |
| April | 30 |
| May | 77 |
| June | 96 |
| July | 118 |
| August | 137 |
| September | 111 |
| October | 215 |
| November | 112 |
| December | 207 |
| | 1185 |

| **1944** | |
|---|---|
| January | 267 |
| February | 315 |
| March | 325 |
| April | 469 |
| May | 417 |
| June | 425 |
| July | 391 |
| August | 340 |
| September | 408 |
| October | 221 |
| November | 247 |
| December | 196 |
| | 4021 |

| **1945** | |
|---|---|
| January | 365 |
| February | 222 |
| March | 309 |
| April | 221 |
| May | 150 |
| | 1277 |

**SUMMARY**

| | |
|---|---|
| 1942 | 50 |
| 1943 | 1185 |
| 1944 | 4021 |
| 1945 | 1277 |
| **TOTAL** | 6533 |

# "MEN OF THE FORTRESS"
Poem by Cpl. Ellsworth B. Laurence
As found in *The Stars and Stripes*

There have been some great traditions
Through a thousand years of kings,
Long centuries of battles fought,
Crusades, campaigns and things-

That gave to many regiments
Traditions tried and true,
Honors aged and multiplied,
As they fought decades through.

The echo of the trumpeter
Whose repertoire at large,
Embraced but one great battle call:
"Forward!  Bayonets!  Charge!"

There's the spirit of the Alamo,
Of courage unsurpassed;
Concord Bridge and San Juan Hill,
Verdun's "They shall not pass!"

Such fighting makes tradition.
But today, unlike the past,
A fledgling code without prelude
Becomes tradition fast,

The Air Force carved its heritage
On the highways of the skies,
Blazing there the fighting code
Of every man who flies.

Yet few know this tradition
The armada built upstairs,
Where the bombers blazing fifties
Defy the flak, and dare

The fighter packs, the rocket bombs
And shell blasts- to attack!
It's a mighty proud tradition
To have "Never been turned back!"

*James J. "Reddo" Redmond, Jr.*

# "TO THE FIGHTERS"
## Poem By Cpl Ellsworth B. Laurence
As found in <u>The Stars and Stripes</u>

There's many a toast to the bombers
That shuttle their lethal might,
So here's glasses high to the fighters,
Who escort them on their flight.

Darting amongst the vapor trails,
Slicing through rockets and flak,
Quick to accept or challenge fight
From enemy fighter pack.

We like to think of the fighter
As a daring tenacious thing
With speed and grace of a humming bird
That packs a cobra's sting!

Of blazing guns and dog fights
Contesting grit and skill,
With utter contempt for danger,
Circling in for the kill!

We like to think of the victories,
The double and triple score!
But let's not forget the fighters might
Is that and something more!

We know they pack a lightning punch
To quench an avenger's thirst
But above and beyond the lust to score,
The Bombers and Target come first!

So when you appraise the fighter,
Think first of the duty he fills
As the armored escort to Bombers,
Then thrill all the more at the kills:

Knowing they've brought the bombers back
You'll affix their "Fighter Score"
As a sort of a plus to their regular job,
It's duty...and something more.

# CONCLUSION

From my generation to yours; these are the stories of my experiences as a B-17 Bomber Pilot and my crew from the start of war in Europe in 1939 to the end of hostilities. The recollections from this period of my life reflect peace-time draft, war-time draft, basic training, life on base, the formation of my crew and the war itself. This is my gift to my children, my grandchildren, great grandchildren and generations yet unborn. History books will not present the details of the lives of the crewmen of the 351st Bomb Group and what they went through during World War II. I feel it is an important aspect of history yet untold. Enjoy my memories...


James J. "Reddo" Redmond, Jr.

Printed in the United States
24172LVS00004B/68

9 781414 031149